PS
561
755
'9
70
D0081616

GARRISON KEILLOR

Photo of Garrison Keillor by Carmen Quesada. Courtesy of Garrison Keillor.

GARRISON KEILLOR

A Critical Companion

Marcia Songer

CRITICAL COMPANIONS TO POPULAR CONTEMPORARY WRITERS
Kathleen Gregory Klein, Series Editor

Greenwood Press
Westport, Connecticut • London

Library of Congress Cataloging-in-Publication Data

Songer, Marcia, 1936–
    Garrison Keillor : a critical companion / by Marcia Songer.
        p.   cm.—(Critical companions to popular contemporary writers, ISSN 1082–4979)
    Includes bibliographical references and index.
    ISBN 0–313–30230–8 (alk. paper)
        1. Keillor, Garrison—Criticism and interpretation.   2. Humorous stories,
American—History and criticism.   3. Pastoral fiction, American—History and
criticism.   4. Lake Wobegon (Minn. : Imaginary place)   5. Minnesota—In literature.
I. Title.   II. Series.
    PS3561.E3755Z89   2000
    813'.54—dc21   99–088460

British Library Cataloguing in Publication Data is available.

Copyright © 2000 by Marcia Songer

All rights reserved. No portion of this book may be
reproduced, by any process or technique, without the
express written consent of the publisher.

Library of Congress Catalog Card Number: 99–088460
ISBN: 0–313–30230–8
ISSN: 1082–4979

First published in 2000

Greenwood Press, 88 Post Road West, Westport, CT 06881
An imprint of Greenwood Publishing Group, Inc.
www.greenwood.com

Printed in the United States of America

The paper used in this book complies with the
Permanent Paper Standard issued by the National
Information Standards Organization (Z39.48–1984).

10 9 8 7 6 5 4 3 2 1

Profuse thanks go to all who helped with this project—to Linda Barker for enthusiastic assistance, to Ryan Otto for dogged persistence, to my husband for unending patience, and to my department for constant support.

ADVISORY BOARD

Mary Catherine Byrd, English Teacher, East Montgomery High School, Biscoe, North Carolina

Dr. Dana McDougald, Library Media Specialist, Cedar Shoals High School, Athens, Georgia

Patricia Naismith, Library Media Specialist, Springfield High School, Springfield, Pennsylvania

Italia Negroni, Head, Library Media Technology Department, Stamford High School, Stamford, Connecticut

Rudy Rocamontes, Jr., English Teacher, Southwest High School, San Antonio, Texas

Alice F. Stern, Young Adults Librarian, Boston Public Library, Boston, Massachusetts

Marcia Welsh, Assistant Director, Guilford Free Library, Guilford, Connecticut

Contents

Series Foreword

The authors who appear in the series Critical Companions to Popular Contemporary Writers are all best-selling writers. They do not simply have one successful novel, but a string of them. Fans, critics, and specialist readers eagerly anticipate their next book. For some, high cash advances and breakthrough sales figures are automatic; movie deals often follow. Some writers become household names, recognized by almost everyone.

But their novels are read one by one. Each reader chooses to start and, more important, to finish a book because of what she or he finds there. The real test of a novel is in the satisfaction its readers experience. This series acknowledges the extraordinary involvement of readers and writers in creating a best-seller.

The authors included in this series were chosen by an Advisory Board composed of high school English teachers and high school and public librarians. They ranked a list of best-selling writers according to their popularity among different groups of readers. For the first series, writers in the top-ranked group who had received no book-length, academic/literary analysis (or none in at least the past ten years) were chosen. Because of this selection method, Critical Companions to Popular Contemporary Writers meets a need that is being addressed nowhere else. The success of these volumes as reported by reviewers, librarians, and teachers led to an expansion of the series mandate to include some writers with wide critical attention—Toni Morrison, John Irving, and Maya Angelou, for example—to extend the usefulness of the series.

The volumes in the series are written by scholars with particular expertise in analyzing popular fiction. These specialists add an academic focus to the popular success these writers already enjoy.

The series is designed to appeal to a wide range of readers. The general reading public will find explanations for the appeal of these well-known writers. Fans will find biographical and fictional questions answered. Students will find literary analysis, discussions of fictional genres, carefully organized introductions to new ways of reading the novels, and bibliographies for additional research. Whether browsing through the book for pleasure or using it for an assignment, readers will find that the most recent novels of the authors are included.

Each volume begins with a biographical chapter drawing on published information, autobiographies or memoirs, prior interviews, and, in some cases, interviews given especially for this series. A chapter on literary history and genres describes how the author's work fits into a larger literary context. The following chapters analyze the writer's most important, most popular, and most recent novels in detail. Each chapter focuses on one or more novels. This approach, suggested by the Advisory Board as the most useful to student research, allows for an in-depth analysis of the writer's fiction. Close and careful readings with numerous examples show readers exactly how the novels work. These chapters are organized around three central elements: plot development (how the story line moves forward), character development (what the reader knows of the important figures), and theme (the significant ideas of the novel). Chapters may also include sections on generic conventions (how the novel is similar to or different from others in its same category of science fiction, fantasy, thriller, etc.), narrative point of view (who tells the story and how), symbols and literary language, and historical or social context. Each chapter ends with an "alternative reading" of the novel. The volume concludes with a primary and secondary bibliography, including reviews.

The alternative readings are a unique feature of this series. By demonstrating a particular way of reading each novel, they provide a clear example of how a specific perspective can reveal important aspects of the book. In the alternative reading sections, one contemporary literary theory—way of reading, such as feminist criticism, Marxism, new historicism, deconstruction, or Jungian psychological critique—is defined in brief, easily comprehensible language. That definition is then applied to the novel to highlight specific features that might go unnoticed or be understood differently in a more general reading. Each volume defines two or three specific theories, making them part of the reader's understanding of how diverse meanings may be constructed from a single novel.

Taken collectively, the volumes in the Critical Companions to Popular Contemporary Writers series provide a wide-ranging investigation of the complexities of current best-selling fiction. By treating these novels seriously as both literary works and publishing successes, the series demonstrates the potential of popular literature in contemporary culture.

Kathleen Gregory Klein
Southern Connecticut State University

1

The Life of Garrison Keillor

The man the world of public radio knows as Garrison Keillor was born Gary Edward Keillor on August 7, 1942, in Anoka, Minnesota. He was the third of six children born to John Philip and Grace Ruth Denham Keillor. John Keillor was a railway mail clerk who augmented his income by doing carpentry. When Gary was five years old, his father purchased property in Brooklyn Park, eight miles from Anoka, and used his carpentry skills to build a house for his growing family. It was in this house that Gary lived until he left for college. Brooklyn Park, like Anoka, is a suburb of Minneapolis today, but it retained rural aspects while he was growing up there. He has fond memories of playing in the nearby fields and streams (Fedo 10).

Other childhood memories are not all pleasant. He was gangly while growing to his adult height of six feet four inches. When he was in the seventh grade, he saw an older boy imitate the loping way in which he walked and was mortified by such mockery (Halvorsen 8B). Gary's understandable embarrassment was intensified by his natural shyness. As an adult, he would be able to joke about that shyness, but as an adolescent, he felt only agony.

His parents belonged to a fundamentalist sect called the Plymouth Brethren. They met in homes and eventually joined a group that gathered in Minneapolis, half an hour away. As with many such groups, the Brethren spent less time emphasizing the fundamentals of their religion than stressing the negatives of the world about them. In order to distinguish themselves from the secular world, they prohibited television in addition to the common evils of drinking, smoking, movies, and dancing. The Brethren did, however, allow their members to use the radio, and Keillor remembers listening with his family ("Portrait" 30). That simple circumstance affected his eventual choice of radio rather than television for *A Prairie Home Companion*, the program that catapulted him to national fame. Even though the family finally got television when Keillor was fourteen, by then he had already developed mixed feelings about the medium (Keillor, "The Boy Who" 42). He was later to tell an interviewer, "Television isolates people even when they're sitting cheek by jowl. Listening to radio, though, is a communal experience" (Hemingson 18).

Keillor's urge to write surfaced early. In grade school he tried publishing newspapers, and at Anoka High School he submitted article after article to the school paper. He was just sixteen when the Anoka *Herald* paid him for an article about a high school football win. Although he continued to report for that newspaper, his parents became concerned about his writing only when some of his poetry was published. That somehow seemed to them shameful (Letofsky 7C).

It was in junior high school that he used the name "Garrison" for the first time. When he submitted poetry to a school literary magazine, he wanted a pen name. "Garrison" seemed like a way to make his own name more formidable (Beyette 2). Later he tried a variant on both his names and used "Garrison Edwards" as a byline for his high school articles (Fedo 18).

After graduating from Anoka High School in 1960, Keillor entered the University of Minnesota. His older brother was the only Keillor to go to college before him. Like many undergraduates, Garrison had a hazy idea of what he wanted to be—a writer—but no clear idea of how to go about becoming one. He had to work to pay his way through school, and one of the jobs he found was at WMMR-AM, a university radio station. He also worked as a parking lot attendant and dishwasher, but he later admitted, "Announcing is much easier than parking cars or washing dishes, and yet it has a kind of status attached to it that I've never understood" (qtd. in Hemingson 18).

Keillor was never an assiduous student, spending much of his time writing and dreaming instead of tending to his lessons. His lack of motivation combined with working resulted in his dropping out of the university in 1962. Once out of school, he found a full-time job on a St. Paul newspaper and worked there for four months, long enough to realize that journalistic writing was not his forte. The paper must have come to the same conclusion because Keillor now thinks that rather than being dropped as temporary help, he was "gently fired" (Beyette 2).

When he returned to the university in 1963, he had a newfound enthusiasm. He worked for KUOM-AM, another university radio station, and he became fiction editor of a literary magazine called the *Ivory Tower*. By 1964 he was *Ivory Tower* editor, a job that carried both status and remuneration. Unfortunately, he had to resign that position in his senior year. He had never retaken classes in which he received grades of *Incomplete*. After a stipulated length of time, they became F's, and when that happened, he was put on academic probation. That was all the warning he needed. He retook the classes and earned A's. He finally graduated from the University of Minnesota in 1966, receiving a bachelor of arts degree in English. By the time he graduated, he had also passed another milestone: on September 11, 1965, he had married Mary Guntzel, a music student at the university.

Following graduation, Garrison hitchhiked east, hoping to get a job with either the *New Yorker* or the *Atlantic*. His longstanding admiration of the *New Yorker* dated to high school when he bought his first copy. At home he had to hide the magazine—his parents would have disapproved of its worldliness (Keillor, *Happy* xi)—but at school he carried it around, showing it off as a badge of sophistication (Scholl, *Garrison* 6). In imitation of E. B. White, he tried signing his name G. E. Keillor (Keillor, *We Are* xiii), and many of the pieces he wrote for the *Ivory Tower* were in imitation of "The Talk of the Town," a regular feature of the *New Yorker*. Desire does not always control destiny, however. Both the *New Yorker* and the *Atlantic* rejected him, and he returned to Minneapolis. There he went back to his job at KUOM-AM and entered graduate school, working toward a master of arts in English, a degree he never finished.

His writing experience during the university years was varied. In 1965 two of his poems won honorable mention in the university's American Academy of Poets Contest. They were published in the *Ivory Tower* as were two more poems the following year when he won first prize. During his association with the magazine, he wrote more poetry, but he also wrote both signed and unsigned articles, short stories, reviews, and editorials. In the prose writing two trends seem distinctive. One is satire of Midwestern middle-class life. In an interview he later admitted that he satirized the wrong things. He said, "I pretended I was a stranger here, that I came from New York and I was commenting on this strange, outlandish behavior of the residents" (Letofsky 7C). In his satire pseudosophistication is the predominant tone, but in other writing one can see the beginning of a second trend, the tone of the small-town resident who comments on his fellows with love as well as humor.

In 1968, after the *Atlantic* published one of his poems, he quit his job at the radio station in order to focus on his writing. It was an action he was to repeat several times more. It gave him the freedom he needed for creative activity, but the birth of his son Jason in 1969 suddenly brought that freedom to an end. It was time to get a paying job again, this time with KSJR-FM, a public radio station run by Minnesota Educational Radio. Even with the responsibilities of a job, marriage, and fatherhood, by 1970 he achieved one of his goals: the *New Yorker* published "Local Family Keeps Son Happy," a funny article that gave rise to some of the Minnesota humor that would follow. He later told his readers, "I've written for *The New Yorker* since I was in high school, though they weren't aware of it at the time" (*We Are* xiii).

That was the beginning of an ongoing relationship with the *New Yorker*. By the time the magazine had published several more of his articles, he found the nerve to try once more to leave radio and make a living from his writing. Again he returned, this time to public radio's new station, KSJN-FM in St. Paul, which plugged his *New Yorker* publications in its promotional material. There he started using *A Prairie Home Companion* as the title of a morning show that combined music, light talk, and fake advertisements. The *Minneapolis Tribune* called it a "low-key, high brow breakfast-hour program" ("Keillor to Quit").

Keillor stayed at KSJN until 1973, when he took one more creative leave. During that time away from the station, he visited the Grand Ole Opry in preparation for writing a *New Yorker* article. For years that Nashville, Tennessee, institution broadcast a live radio show of country music and humor. As he sat in the audience, Keillor thought, "I could do that" (qtd. in Bunce 36). Shortly after he returned to KSJN in 1974, he launched an evening version of *A Prairie Home Companion*. Like the Opry, it was broadcast on Saturday night; within two months it was also broadcast live.

There were only fifteen people in the audience of that first live performance although the Janet Wallace Concert Hall where it was held seated four hundred ("What's Up"). The producer Margaret Moos was so embarrassed that she moved the show to an eighty-two-seat theater, which the audience soon filled. Within a few years 650 people were watching the show at the World Theater every Saturday night, and more attended special outdoor versions of the show (Ingrassia 1).

The number of listeners also continued to grow. In 1977 Minnesota Public Radio, which Minnesota Educational Radio had become in 1974, recognized Keillor's popularity and collected his writing in a publication called *G. K. the DJ*. The network offered it during a fund drive as an incentive to subscribers. As MPR added stations to its network, *A Prairie Home Companion* gained a wider radio audience. Nevertheless, it was an audience largely confined to Minnesota until 1979 when the Minnesota network joined other public stations to form American Public Radio and to offer original programming to other stations nationwide. *A Prairie Home Companion* was the centerpiece of its offerings. In May 1980 the first satellite broadcast of the two-hour evening program hit the airwaves. Suddenly the humor of Minnesota was being heard all across the country, and public radio listeners in all states were becoming familiar with Lake Wobegon, "where all the women are strong, all the men are good-looking, and all the children are above average." That October the show won the George Foster Peabody Award for excellence in broadcasting.

The weekly evening broadcast followed a format similar to the one Keillor had used on the morning version. Instead of recorded music, however, the music also was live. In addition to the Butch Thompson trio, which appeared as a mainstay, he invited folk, bluegrass, and jazz musicians, choirs, even opera singers to appear as guest performers. Often they joined him in duets, which might be religious songs, traditional songs, or parodies. One writer called the music a "mix of bluegrass, Bach and bumpkin" (Lague 44). As a morning disk jockey, Keillor had been criticized for deviating from the classical agenda. Now the evening show was attacked by some classical music lovers who claimed it did not belong on public radio. Some managers, however, carried it specifically to counter accusations that public radio is elitist (Ingrassia 15).

Keillor expanded the ads on the evening show to include Ralph's Pretty Good Grocery and Bob's Bank. Because Keillor describes himself as shy, an important sponsor was Powdermilk Biscuits, which "give shy persons the strength to get up and do what needs to be done." Soon MPR was selling baseball caps featuring the Lake Wobegon Whippets, T-shirts from Bertha's Kitty Boutique, and dishtowels from the Lutheran Church Basement Women.

In his broadcasts Keillor interspersed humorous sketches with songs, ads, and some conversation with the audience, but the highlight of each program was the monologue. It invariably began, "It has been a quiet week in Lake Wobegon, my home town." Originally lasting only a few minutes, the monologue lengthened and developed into a familiar feature predictably occurring after the midpoint in the program. The monologues became so popular that in 1983 Minnesota Public Radio released a set of four tapes called "News from Lake Wobegon." The set reproduced twenty monologues divided according to the seasons. Because a previous tape had included skits, ads, and songs, confining this set to just the monologues indicates how important they had become.

One writer described the monologues as "an eccentric combination of comedy routine, literary storytelling and essay" (Graham). Some were hilarious, but in others Keillor had "the courage not to be funny" (Skow, "Lonesome" 70), talking instead about loneliness or the pain of growing up. The appeal of the monologues is sometimes attributed to a nostalgic longing for the small-town past of many Americans, but that idea does not explain the popularity among listeners on the Australian Broadcasting Corporation or fans who have always lived in cities. Rather the monologues ring true for many people who have never been to the American Midwest because they seem personal and extemporaneous. In fact, they result from careful planning and writing even though the delivery is made with no script. Keillor explained in an interview that people "don't want to know that there has been work done, because people believe in spontaneity." They feel that "writing represents something artificial" while the monologue "represents something that is spontaneous and therefore more truthful and good" (Bunce 36). Keillor admits that going out with no notes "makes it possible . . . to do monologues that are sometimes flat." However, he adds, "People forgive that because the ones that move them, move them very much" (Roback, "*PW* Interviews" 138).

In 1981 Atheneum published *Happy to Be Here*, a collection of short pieces, most of which had already appeared in the *New Yorker* or elsewhere. The book became a best-seller, and the proceeds enabled Keillor to buy his first home (Bream 6). He had returned to his morning show in 1976, dividing his time between it and the evening show. With the success of the latter, he once again wanted more time to write, and on April 12, 1982, he resigned from the morning program. Then he set about revising and enlarging *Happy to Be Here* for a paperback version that came out in 1983.

By 1984, when *A Prairie Home Companion* celebrated its tenth anniversary, the show was carried by 235 stations and had become public radio's most effective fund-raiser. Nick Coleman, writing for the *Minneapolis Star and Tribune*, called Keillor the "Jimmy Swaggart of the yumpie set," defining *yumpie* as "young, urban, upwardly mobile professional" (1G). In his opinion, people gave generously because they wanted public radio to spread "The Gospel according to Garrison" (1G). Coleman contended that Keillor's message, though secular, resembled the sermon of a religious fundamentalist in that he prompted people to look inward at their own foolishness and failings (10G).

At the time of the anniversary, the show was temporarily being produced in the Orpheum Theatre while the World underwent renovations. Articles lauding the show pointed out changes over the years: Keillor had discarded his beard and hat even though he retained his white suit and red socks; the format had evolved and matured. Despite winning two Corporation for Public Broadcasting Awards, the program had not lost its homey feel, and Keillor could say of it, "We still do it . . . for our own amusement" (qtd. in Bream 5).

He continued to write for the *New Yorker* and the *Atlantic*, and he began to write *Lake Wobegon Days*, which dealt with the same material as his monologues. *The Atlantic* carried a prepublication preview of the book in August 1985, and shortly after it was published in October, it became a Book-of-the-Month Club selection. It made the *New York Times* best-seller list and stayed there for more than a year. By that time the radio audience had grown to two million (Beyette 2), and tickets for seats in the theater audience were sold out far in advance. In November *Time* featured him on its cover. There was no question that fame had found Garrison Keillor.

Yet the year 1985 was important to Keillor for another reason. He and Mary Guntzel Keillor had been divorced in 1976. While attending the twenty-fifth reunion of the Anoka High School class of 1960, he renewed acquaintance with a former classmate, Ulla Strange Skaerved. An exchange student from Denmark, Ulla corresponded with Keillor for several years after their graduation, but they eventually lost touch. When they met again at the reunion, Keillor was smitten. Although Keillor seemed annoyed at press reports of their courtship, he frequently alluded to it himself when he was on the air, and he told a St. Paul paper, "She thinks of me as passionate and sweet and a terrific singer, which is what I have wanted to be all my life" (qtd. in "Lake Wobegon's Garrison"). On December 29, 1985, they were married in Holte, Denmark.

The marriage affected more than his private life. Margaret Moos, his former companion and the longtime producer of *A Prairie Home Companion*, left the show. By the spring of 1986, regular performers Butch

Thompson and Peter Oustroushko also left. On Valentine's Day 1987 came the announcement that Keillor too would leave. After a thirteen-year run, he said that it was time to go, that he and Ulla would be moving to Denmark for a while. He explained to his audience, "I want to resume the life of a shy person and live with my affectionate family a more peaceful life. I'm tired. And it's time to stop" (qtd. in Barol 65). Typical of fan reaction was that of Tom Brokaw of NBC News: "I'm a grown-up so I know things come to an end. . . . But it's going to leave a void" (qtd. in Galant).

Disney televised the show the last few months, a fact that Keillor, with his ambivalence toward television, regretted after he gave permission (Keillor, *We Are* 158). Nevertheless, for many who lived too far from Minneapolis to ever be part of a live audience, it was possible to see Keillor for the first time. His customary red socks and tie or suspenders inevitably surprised first-time viewers. Since the radio audience could not see him, the costume had been only for the benefit of those who were actually in attendance at the broadcasts. It is one more indication of the importance both audiences have always played in Keillor's performances. In fact, the radio show used separate audio mixes for the radio and auditorium audiences (Sutin 45). From the February 14 announcement through the last performance on June 13, 1987, all 925 seats in the renovated World Theater were filled ("A Home Companion" 39). Televising the show in no way reduced the audience's desire to be there in person.

Following the final performance, the Keillors left for Denmark so that he "could be the foreigner in the family" (Keillor, "Intriguers" 82). He admitted that he was fleeing from celebrity (Barol 82). He had been particularly angry with local newspapers for publishing the address of his St. Paul home and pursuing him and Ulla unmercifully. In his eyes they seemed to be punishing him for being successful (Meier 8A). He later wrote that the experience taught him what the prodigal son's brother discovered, that people love those who fail and excoriate those who succeed, and woe be to any who complain (*We Are* 143).

Once in Copenhagen he relished being able to walk around without being recognized. He studied Danish and had plans for writing a screenplay. He read and wrote, but he also grew frustrated at having to use only the rudiments of a language. He later compared the experience to "living the immigrant dream in reverse, starting with success in America, then the voyage, then the life of servitude in the Old World" (*Leaving* xiii). Soon he realized "it was time to come back" (Barol 83). The Denmark hiatus lasted until September 1987 when he and Ulla returned to the United States, and he began working as a staff writer for the *New Yorker*.

Because Ulla was as uncomfortable in St. Paul as he had been in Copenhagen, New York became a suitable compromise, but moving there also realized a youthful dream of Keillor's. At eighteen, like one of his characters in *Lake Wobegon Days*, he had made a list of things one should do to become a writer. Living in New York was one of them (Levin 36).

The year 1987 was also important for two notable achievements. Keillor received a Grammy award for best spoken-word recording for *Lake Wobegon Days*, a set of cassette tapes, and he published *Leaving Home*, a collection of radio monologues adapted for print. The book uses characters already familiar to the reader, but all the stories deal with some form of leaving. The last of the stories is the monologue Keillor gave on his good-bye broadcast. Although the title seems foreknowing, Keillor claims he was unaware, when he chose it, that he too would be leaving (Roback, "Leaving" 34). Like *Lake Wobegon Days* the book became a selection of the Book-of-the-Month Club, and Viking was so sure of its success that it ran a prepublication second printing.

In the meantime Minnesota Public Radio had tried to replace *A Prairie Home Companion* with a new production called *Good Evening*. It used the same Saturday evening time slot and starred Noah Adams, who for five years had hosted National Public Radio's *All Things Considered*. That popular news program had three million listeners compared to the four million on two hundred stations that *A Prairie Home Companion* had at the time of its departure (Bowermaster 45). There was no attempt to imitate Keillor but instead to try another live show with a variety format. Nevertheless, comparisons were inevitable, and despite favorable reviews, the show struggled.

In May 1989 American Public Radio announced that *Good Evening* would be shortened and Keillor would return. By November he was on the air again, this time from New York. As before, the show was a two-hour live program broadcast on Saturday evenings, but it was called *The American Radio Company of the Air*, and there were some differences. The music was more sophisticated, less because it emanated from the Brooklyn Academy of Music than because the folk/country elements Keillor had favored in Minneapolis seemed out of place in New York. The new skits also had an urban flavor even though Keillor still sang and did a monologue. Meanwhile he continued in his job at the *New Yorker*, leading one commentator to observe that "there's a war going on in the man about whether he's a man of letters—a theatrical Thurber perhaps—or a man of public radio" (Bromberg A12). *We Are Still Married*, published in 1989, is a collection of pieces written for the *New Yorker* and a few other magazines.

During the three years that *The American Radio Company of the Air* broadcast from New York, only rarely did Keillor mention Lake Wobegon. He told a reporter in Atlanta it seemed "cruel" to talk to an audience in Brooklyn about life in a small town (Graham). Instead he tried various approaches in his humor. Some skits used the impressions of the newcomer who sees the city with naiveté; others, the view of the hardened resident who might as well laugh at some of the city's drawbacks. He sometimes seemed defensive about not returning to the Midwest, but most of his energy was focused on finding the right mix of elements to make the show in New York the resounding success it had been in St. Paul.

Successful it was, although not as successful as *A Prairie Home Companion*, and eventually Keillor decided to take the show back to Minnesota. He returned to the World Theater in the fall of 1992 with plans to broadcast eighteen shows from St. Paul, ten from New York, and an unspecified number on the road. He explained the move by saying, "I like the city—I could talk for an hour about it. But most of the people I know really well live back in Minnesota, and as you get older you don't make friends as easily" (qtd. in Nelson and Stansbury 8A). His ambivalence about New York versus the Midwest was apparent in his living arrangements: he built a cabin in western Wisconsin but kept his New York apartment.

The first year back in St. Paul Keillor kept the program as *The American Radio Company*, but in 1993 he revived the name and format of *A Prairie Home Companion*. Thus it remains, but with some differences. He has some new fake sponsors, duct tape among them, and new skits, and the show has moved to the Fitzgerald Theatre. The monologue, however, has returned to Lake Wobegon, to the joy of most listeners. Occasionally Butch Thompson and Peter Oustroushko come back too. Nonetheless, Keillor returns to New York every year when he takes the show on the road. His technical director says New York "gets his creative juices going" (Vecsey C1). In addition, the talent pool there is unlimited. After a show that featured two opera singers, Keillor explained, "I don't think they would have come out to Minnesota just to sing a few songs" (qtd. in Vecsey C24).

Much of Keillor's most visible success is due to his radio show, now heard by 2.2 million listeners on more than 410 public radio stations ("Garrison," Online). He has won the Edward R. Murrow Award, two ACE awards, and a medal from the American Academy of Letters. His recording of *Lake Wobegon Days* won a Grammy, and in 1994 he was inducted into the Radio Hall of Fame. For many years tapes and CDs of his monologues have been available in *Signal* and *Wireless* catalogs. Now *A Prairie Home Companion* has mall stores and a catalog of its own. In addition, Keillor's monologues are used to help nonnative speakers learn conversational English (Boyd and Quinn).

Yet Garrison Keillor, the writer, has not deferred to Garrison Keillor, the radio performer. In fact, when Keillor returned to Anoka High School to give the commencement address in June 1990, he thanked the town for giving him the "sense of belonging and the insecurity he needed to be a writer" (Halvorsen 1B). He stressed his writing, not his performance. Since the publication of *Happy to Be Here* in 1981, he has released a new book every two years. In 1991 the new work was *WLT: A Radio Romance*. That was followed by *The Book of Guys* in 1993; a children's book, *Cat, You Better Come Home* in 1995; and *Wobegon Boy* in 1997.

In September of 1992, Tina Brown left *Vanity Fair* to take over the helm of the *New Yorker*. When Keillor heard that she was to become the new editor, he abruptly quit. In an interview with George Plimpton, he explained that he was familiar with other magazines she had edited and knew the magazine would change drastically. He felt she would not be interested in anything he might write (115–16). Instead he turned his attention to other projects. He currently does some writing for *Time* and for the internet magazine *Salon*, and in 1993 he began a new public radio program, *The Writer's Almanac*. In a daily five-minute segment, he gives birthdays and other important literary events that occurred on that day. Then he closes by reading a poem. The program seems symbolic. He uses the medium of radio, but the people he honors are writers.

In his private life Keillor, having divorced Ulla Skaerved in 1991, is now married to violinist Jenny Lind Nilsson, who gave birth to a baby girl on December 29, 1997. The Keillors named the baby Maia Grace Keillor. Grace is for Keillor's mother, but Maia is the name of one of the Pleiades, the daughters of Atlas. The month of May is named for her, and ancient Romans annually held a celebration in her honor to guarantee good crops.

Keillor admitted concern about becoming a father again at age fifty-five, but the joy of that moment he shared on the *Prairie Home Companion* web site. He described holding his new daughter as "a religious experience, one to remember forever" and proclaimed the holiday two days later "the most wonderful New Year's Eve" of his life ("A Little Girl"). Fans hope the name chosen for the newest Keillor is indicative that Garrison Keillor will be productive for years to come.

2

Keillor's Literary Heritage

Garrison Keillor is known as a humorist, someone who specializes in humor. "Humor," however, is a word of many meanings. *Webster's Collegiate Dictionary* gives as definitions "something that is or is designed to be comical and amusing" and "that quality which appeals to a sense of the ludicrous or absurdly incongruous" ("Humor"). *A Handbook to Literature* addresses the history of the word and distinguishes between wit and humor. As the terms are used today, "*wit* is primarily intellectual . . . and is expressed in skillful phraseology, plays on words, surprising contrasts, paradoxes, epigrams, and so forth, whereas *humor* implies a sympathetic recognition of human values and deals with the foibles and incongruities of human nature, good-naturedly exhibited" (Harmon and Holman). According to that distinction, Keillor displays both wit and humor in much of his writing.

From the Greeks who laughed at Aristophanes' *Lysistrata* during the Golden Age to the Americans who chuckle at Jay Leno's quips today, people have long enjoyed humor. Although humor can be negative if it comes at the expense of the innocent, it is a very positive force when the subject is appropriate. Laughter can provide relief and release; it can divert the weary and uplift the depressed. In *The Comic Vision in Literature* Edward L. Galligan says of humor, "If it does not make you laugh or smile it has failed. Yet laughter is not its only goal, . . . for humor is greatly concerned with the meanings uncovered by its jokes" (17). Galligan goes on to explain that whatever makes people laugh also makes them think.

It is important to Garrison Keillor to make people think as well as laugh. In his satire, he follows the time-honored purpose of the form: to ridicule those people and institutions whose failings are correctable. He draws on a comic tradition that, in America, dates back to Benjamin Franklin. Franklin is known for humorous essays such as "Remarks Concerning the Savages of North America." In that work Franklin uses the word "savages" ironically. He describes an offer made by Virginians to educate six young men of the Iroquois tribes. With extreme politeness the tribal representative declines the offer, citing as an example young men previously given the "opportunity" of an education. They returned without the skills necessary to survive within the Iroquois community. They could neither hunt nor build a cabin; they could not kill an enemy or serve as a counselor. In short, "they were totally good for nothing" (220). Nevertheless, the speaker shows gratitude for the offer by proposing to take a dozen young Virginians and instruct them in the ways of the Iroquois.

Elsewhere in the article, Franklin tells of a minister who preaches the message of Christian salvation to the chiefs of the Susquehanna Indians. In response, one of the chiefs recounts the myth of a beautiful maiden who gave the Indians maize, kidney beans, and tobacco. When the minister conveys disgust at what he considers superstitious lies, the Indian is offended at the minister's ignorance of "the rules of common civility." He concludes, "You saw that we, who understand and practice those rules, believed all your stories; why do you refuse to believe ours?" (221).

Many of the short pieces Keillor wrote originally for the *New Yorker* have a similar ironic tone. In "Jack Schmidt, Arts Administrator" the admiring elevator operator speaks of Jack's "spirit of inquiry" as a private detective (*Happy* 19). Such use of word play abounds in Keillor's work, but more reminiscent of Franklin is Keillor's satire. He pokes fun at the smugness of political leaders in such essays as "The New Washington: An Inside Story" and "U.S. Still on Top, Says Rest of World," both collected in *Happy to Be Here*. In "The New Washington" a cabinet member in the Reagan administration is convinced that the rest of the nation looks at the glamorous Washington lifestyle with admiration, only hoping to one day be worthy of sharing such a life. He never once thinks the capital's conspicuous display inappropriate even though at that time much of the country is in recession. In "U.S. Still on Top," it is President Nixon himself who is bragging about the superior position of the nation.

He says the country is in first place in the world, but he does not say in what. Keillor puts the statement in perspective by making it seem to be derived from a popularity contest. The pieces make fun of quotes from politicians who, like Franklin's Virginians, have an assumption of superiority.

Franklin looks beyond common perceptions to recognize the quality of Indians whom others dismiss as savages. In "How the Savings and Loans Were Saved," one of the pieces in *We Are Still Married*, Keillor turns the tables and regards as savages those whom others have admired. His savages are savings and loan executives who bilked innocent people out of their life savings. He portrays the executives as Huns invading Chicago, where their uncivilized behavior includes building campfires in offices and eating partially cooked meat. Like Franklin, Keillor looks under the veneer seen by society to find the common quality beneath. In the case of the executives, it is primitive greed.

In his nonsatirical writing Keillor finds humor in universals with which his audience can identify. Galligan says, "Comedy concerns those life and death matters that all of us must cope with through most of our lives—sex and dying, aggression and injustice, love and vanity, rationality and sense" (xi). Those life and death matters form the basis of much of Keillor's humor and account for his lasting popularity. According to biographer Peter A. Scholl, Keillor's "humor comes from his awareness of death's reality, but death vanquished by laughter in the comic moment and in the promise of eternal regeneration" ("Garrison Keillor and the News" 227). In a monologue called "Collection" in *Leaving Home*, Clarence Bunsen, one of Keillor's favorite Lake Wobegon characters, translates unusual pain into a portent of death. When he realizes he is not having a heart attack, Clarence thinks it is time to reassess his values. He considers buying new underwear, alters his breakfast diet, and wonders whether he should even bother to go to church. He recalls the time in his life when responsibilities for his children kept him from thinking "grim thoughts about death" (81). Keillor uses the story to evoke humor about Norwegians who always claim to be all right despite dire circumstances. He ridicules church members who seem to take their only pleasure in finding fault with others. But Clarence's anxiety about his mortality is everyone's anxiety. Clearly Keillor is concerned about Clarence and people like him. He told one reporter, "Comedy that doesn't care about the world doesn't interest me. . . . there's a whole streak in comedy that is cruel, that picks on weaker people. But it's false comedy" (qtd. in Klose K4).

In the nineteenth century emerged what is now called cracker-barrel humor. The term came from the stories or maxims told by a rustic to a group of men gathered around a cracker barrel in a country store. This humor started in the Midwest and was typified by the use of dialect and the ability of the untutored, sometimes uncouth rustic to make insightful observations. Analyst Judith Lee says, "Unlike a teacher, parent, or other personages in a role superior to the audience's, cracker-barrel philosophers derive their moral authority from personal experience and the innate virtue of their ideas, not from book-learning, social status, or professional standing" (ix). By the twentieth century cracker-barrel humor took many different forms. In Brown County, Indiana, Kin Hubbard created Abe Martin, whose proverbs and cartoon likeness appeared in more than three hundred newspapers (Yates 102). Finley Peter Dunne's Mr. Dooley lived in Chicago, but his immigrant dialect and his commentaries on and to his small Irish neighborhood made him the urban equivalent of the rural sage. Langston Hughes placed his version of the cracker-barrel philosopher, Jess B. Semple, in Harlem.

The best known of the cracker-barrel humorists is Will Rogers, the Oklahoma cowboy who ended up on Broadway swinging a lariat and commenting on the passing scene. Keillor has often been compared to Will Rogers (Beyette 2, Wilbers 6), but it is primarily in his role as radio entertainer that the comparison becomes legitimate. The cracker-barrel influence can be observed in Keillor as host, announcer, and raconteur on *A Prairie Home Companion*. In his down-home, easy voice, he ridicules the latest silliness in political, cultural, or business circles. In addition to affecting the cracker-barrel delivery in his own performance, he gives it to Dad Benson, a radio personality who figures in one story in *Happy to Be Here* and throughout *WLT: A Radio Romance*.

Nevertheless, except for the Benson connection, there is little resemblance between Keillor's writing and that of Will Rogers. Almost all of Rogers's writing takes the form of collections of quips from his stage performances. Norris Yates tells how newspapers tried to get him to write weekly features, but he could neither create characters nor write narratives. He succeeded only when he reverted to writing "epigrams and brief paragraphs, much as he had done orally" (115). In addition, although Rogers pretended to have less education than he really did have, he did not have to pose as an unsophisticated speaker. He deprecated good grammar, good literature, good art. He wrote from Rome, "I don't care anything about Oil Paintings. . . . I don't want to see a lot of old Pictures. If I wanted to see old Pictures I would get D. W. Griffith to revive the Birth of a Nation" (72). He seemed to think the more un-cultured he was, the more impressive his wisdom would seem. Keillor, on the other hand, can write with great sophistication, and his knowl-edge of literature and the arts comes through in all that he does. He may poke fun at avant garde extremists and far-out movements, but his re-gard for classical artists is sincere. Music seems to be the only one of the arts in which his taste is uneducated. Nevertheless, though he obviously prefers country and folk music, he tries to compensate by having some opera singers and other serious musicians as guests on his show.

Another nineteenth-century influence often mentioned in connection with Keillor is local color. Scholl calls Keillor "a brilliant vernacular yarn-spinner and an acute local color observer and nostalgic realist of the Upper Midwest" ("Garrison" 338). Local color can be defined as writing "marked by dialect, eccentric characters, and sentimentalized pathos or whimsical humor" (Harmon and Holman). Its early practitioners were such writers as Bret Harte, Sarah Orne Jewett, and Joel Chandler Harris. They were thought to be accurate in presenting realistic detail of a region without dealing with the universal truths that underlie great literature. Many of the critics who consider Keillor a local colorist make that judg-ment based only on the Lake Wobegon material. In it he certainly does use dialect. *A Prairie Home Companion* has even done skits on How to Speak Minnesotan. He also uses local characteristics and eccentricities as the ba-sis of his jokes. One such characteristic is low self-esteem. Keillor ex-plained in an interview, "Minnesota humor is self-denigrating humor. . . . We try to accuse ourselves of things before other people can get around to it" (qtd. in Beyette 2).

The least desirable of the traits, "sentimentalized pathos," is seldom present in Keillor's work. People who have heard only a few broadcasts of *A Prairie Home Companion* may think them sentimental, and some broadcasts may indeed produce wistful longing in some listeners, but most reveal a small town that is anything but sentimentalized. Instead, Keillor shows "the little town that time forgot" as a victim of its own isolation. If listeners react with nostalgia, they may be like the out-of-town subscribers of the local paper, the *Herald-Star*. They can afford to feel sentimental about Lake Wobegon because they do not have to live there.

The writer to whom Keillor is most frequently compared is Mark Twain, another local color writer from the heartland who transcended the label. William Dean Howells, in reviewing *Roughing It*, Twain's ac-count of an overland stage trip, writes that Twain used "the truest colors that could have been used, for all existence there must have looked like an extravagant joke, the humor of which was only deepened by its nether-side of tragedy" (113). Lee compares the organization of *Lake Wobegon Days* to that of *Tom Sawyer*. Both works "structure their large narratives around anecdotal episodes" (120). She also notes the similarity between the "naive tale-teller" of Keillor's "The Slim Graves Show" and the gullible narrator of Twain's "The Celebrated Jumping Frog of Calaveras County" (124). She points out that both Twain and Keillor use the stock story of a man who gets lost in a blizzard outside his own door, Keillor in "Friendly Neighbor" and Twain in *Roughing It* (132).

Critic Cliff Radel calls the tales from Lake Wobegon "Mark Twainian in scope." He says they are "rich with the bittersweet stuff of life" (B9). Keillor disparaged such comparisons in an early interview, noting that the Twain resemblance is "probably bestowed on four or five people every year by 40 or 50 newspaper reviewers" (qtd. in Beyette 20). Nevertheless, John Skow of *Time* noticed that Keillor often performed in a white suit as did Twain and thought the attire might indicate that Keillor was courting such an association ("Lonesome" 69). Keillor admits that he admires Twain. He once commented, "He's still funny. Twain's after-dinner speeches still make you laugh out loud" (qtd. in Klose K4). Lee has observed that the "distinction between the public and private Keillors, between performer and author, is as blurred as the distinction between Samuel Clemens and Mark Twain, but Keillor apparently likes it that way" (9–10). She goes on to point out that "Keillor and Twain probably resemble each other most in their ability to market themselves as public and commercial properties" (10).

Often people compare Keillor to both Rogers and Twain. One humorous *New York Times* article purported to interview the three men about their attitudes toward the economy and finance. The "answers" of Rogers and Twain were taken from their writings while Keillor was actually interviewed (Pedersen-Pieterson). On another occasion Keillor himself referred to both men when asked how he would be remembered in seventy years. He contrasted the timeliness of Rogers's jokes and the timelessness of Twain's humor (Austin 4–5). With only the radio audience and public appearances to perpetuate fame, Keillor might go the way of Rogers, whose fame diminishes as public memory fades. However, like Twain, his legacy will ultimately depend not on his performances but on his writing.

Also, like Twain, he is not afraid to use his writing to take America to task. Twain himself says that many writers are forgotten because they were "merely humorists." He explains, "Humor must not professedly teach, and it must not professedly preach, but it must do both if it would live forever" (202). Twain goes on to admit that he has always preached. A case in point is the famous scene in *Huckleberry Finn* when Huck struggles with his conscience as he writes a letter. The law says he must report Jim, his companion on a trip down the Mississippi, as a runaway slave. He has been taught that it is his Christian duty to obey the law, and he truly thinks he will go to hell if he does not write to Jim's owner. Yet his natural sense of justice will not allow him to turn in someone with whom he has shared the peril of the river. He has grown to accept Jim as a man, not a slave. There is wry humor in his decision to tear up the letter and risk perdition, but Twain's sermon is clear: Huck's instinctive morality is superior to the morality of pious slaveholders.

To teach his most important lessons, Mark Twain uses an outcast, a boy who lives in a barrel. Keillor too uses outcasts for some of his sermons. Among them are welfare recipients, women whose return to Lake Wobegon when their marriages failed has left them open to the contempt of the community. In *Leaving Home* two monologues, "Eloise" and "The Royal Family," tell of such women and their spunky defiance of Lake Wobegon norms. At other times Keillor uses sympathetic portrayals of clergy, Father Emil of Our Lady of Perpetual Responsibility and David Ingqvist of Lake Wobegon Lutheran, to illustrate the hypocrisy of the religious communities they serve. Keillor condemns the rigidity of small town life in a chapter of *Lake Wobegon Days* called "News." In it a native son indicts the complacency of the small town as a whole and his parents in particular.

For all the similarities, Twain is not the only Midwesterner to whom Keillor is compared. Steven Wilbers says, "Keillor invites comparison with an earlier Midwesterner, James Thurber, and with the late E. B. White" (6). Keillor has to be gratified by that comparison. In the introduction to his first book, *Happy to Be Here*, he tells of his great admiration for the *New Yorker* and what he calls its "great infield of Thurber, Liebling, Perelman and White" (11, Rev. Ed.). He refers to them as his heroes, and he was particularly proud when he eventually followed in their footsteps in first getting published by and then actually becoming a staff writer for that magazine. Just recently Keillor edited a collection of Thurber's writings and drawings.

Thurber hailed from Columbus, Ohio. After working for various publications, he eventually settled in at the *New Yorker* where he alternated with E. B. White in writing "Talk of the Town," a regular feature of the magazine. In his stories, Thurber is best known for his creation of the Little Man, who is cowed by everything from contemporary society to his own wife. Garrison Keillor has created no Walter Mitty, arguably Thurber's best-known character, but he does produce people baffled by various aspects of their lives. One such is Lyle, who appears in "Winter" in *Lake Wobegon Days* and in "Lyle's Roof" in *Leaving Home*. Lyle is the brother-in-law of Carl Krebsbach, to whom no household or automotive task is too difficult. A native of California, Lyle cannot seem to get his car started on extremely cold mornings. Inevitably, Carl starts it for him just as he fixes Lyle's sink and helps fix the roof. Carl's competence makes Lyle feel inadequate. Lyle is overwhelmed by the responsibilities of rearing four children and maintaining a home on a high school teacher's salary. He is frightened of winter in Minnesota and worries that someone, perhaps Carl or perhaps some older man who lives alone, will go mad from the cold and start killing people. Lyle is surely a Little Man. It is not surprising that he has no last name.

Because his wife never enters the stories, Lyle does not fit the mold of the henpecked husband so popular with Thurber, but Keillor creates characters who do. Florian Krebsbach is as sufficiently dominated by his wife Myrtle as any Thurber husband. In "The Secret Life of Walter Mitty" Mitty gets ordered around by a traffic policeman and a parking attendant, but their bossiness is minimal compared to his wife's. Mitty escapes into daydreams in which he is capable and decisive, the one who gives the orders instead of the one who takes them. Like Mitty, Florian tries to avoid confrontation with his wife. In "High Rise," another *Leaving Home* monologue, he escapes by going to tell jokes to his ducks.

Thurber devotes much of his writing to the relationship between men and women. Norris Yates says that Thurber's humor "quivers with sex and with the tensions related thereto" (281). The tensions are particularly evident in Thurber's drawings, such as "The War Between Men and Women" in *Men, Women and Dogs*. Keillor injects similar tensions into the monologues about the Krebsbachs, but other Keillor characters have problems in their marriages too. When the characters are David and Judith Ingqvist, the Lutheran minister and his wife, connubial stress is aggravated by the fact that the congregation expects their marriage to be a model for the whole community. In *Leaving Home* the Ingqvists figure in several of the collected monologues, and they always seem to be having difficulty. In "Pontoon Boat" Judith is shocked to hear of the imminent arrival of a busload of ministers. She makes it clear that neglecting to tell her is not an easily excused offence. Since David did not give her time to plan, he can manage to feed them on his own. She will not compensate for his oversight. At the end of "Exiles," when the Hjalmar Ingqvist family arrives unexpectedly, David and Judith are in the middle of an argument. In "New Year's" Judith is tired of being expected to sit in a prominent pew and look up admiringly at her husband as he gives his sermons. She is tired of hearing him misquote her. She is tired of having no confidante since her friend Katy was practically run out of town for being too frank about the community's shortcomings. Both she and David are exhausted by being always on stage where they must be unremittingly civil to each other. They need respite from Lake Wobegon, its frigid weather, and its equally frigid parishioners. Theirs may not be an all-out Thurberesque war, but the Ingqvists certainly have skirmishes.

With the strides made by feminists, the battle lines of the gender wars have moved from the marriage bed into the workplace. Keillor handles the new tension in "What Did We Do Wrong?" In that story, which appears in *We Are Still Married*, Annie Szemanski tries to become an accepted player in major league baseball. She does not succeed. Then in *The Book of Guys*, Keillor's introduction includes stories of Guy Pride and male bonding in response to feminine strides in many fields. Many of the pieces are spoofs aimed at males who feel threatened by female advances. Nevertheless, the reader feels that, as with Thurber, there is some sincere concern behind the laughter.

Subject is not the only similarity Keillor has with Thurber. Thurber and E. B. White collaborated on a parody of psychological self-help manuals, calling theirs *Is Sex Necessary?* Keillor's *Happy to Be Here* is filled with similar parodies—of newspaper columns, comics, flyers, and brochures. Closest to the Thurber and White effort are his parodies of bestselling books, *My Mother, Myself* and the *Foxfire* series. Although Keillor writes short pieces rather than books, the subjects of the parodies are easily recognized. When he later began writing the "Talk of the Town" column for the *New Yorker*, Keillor's bond with Thurber and White became even stronger.

Garrison Keillor has drawn on his literary heritage to develop two kinds of humor. The one, found in the Lake Wobegon of broadcast and print, harks back to the cracker barrel and local color artists while the other, found in his witty and satirical pieces, shows the influence of Enlightenment and *New Yorker* predecessors. That Keillor is adept at both indicates the breadth of his talent and his stature as a writer.

3

Happy to Be Here
(1981)

Garrison Keillor's first book, *Happy to Be Here*, is a collection of short pieces, most of which appeared in magazines between 1969 and 1981, the year the book was published. Of the twenty-nine compositions in the hardback edition, twenty-six were written for the *New Yorker* while "Your Transit Commission" was first published in the *Atlantic*. To the paperback edition of *Happy to Be Here*, published in 1983, Keillor added five additional pieces: "The Tip-Top Club," "Jack Schmidt on the Burning Sands," "The New Washington: An Inside Story," "My Stepmother, Myself," and "After a Fall." All five appeared first in magazines.

In the introduction Keillor says that he wrote all of the pieces in Minnesota, his birthplace. His writing frequently mirrors the Midwest in general and Minnesota in particular. Nevertheless, it has no difficulty appealing to the sophisticated readers of the *New Yorker*. Keillor's ability to focus with humor on what is commonly called "the human condition" makes his writing relevant to all.

Happy to Be Here is divided into five parts, the compositions in each part being loosely related by subject matter but each standing alone as a story or commentary. Besides adding pieces to the revised edition, Keillor changed their order. Thus, for purposes of clarity, all references here are to the more inclusive revised edition.

PLOT DEVELOPMENT

Most of the pieces in Part One fall into the category of short stories, such as the Jack Schmidt accounts and "Don: The True Story of a Young Person." Jack Schmidt is a former private eye who, after demands for his detective services fall off, turns for a living to finding support for artists. Jack tells how this came about in "Jack Schmidt, Arts Administrator." His love interest at the time, an actress named Trixie, complains that the acting studio where she studies is to be closed due to lack of funding. Jack gets money for the studio, thinking this accomplishment will impress Trixie. Instead, after accepting the money from him, Trixie accuses him of being materialistic and takes up with a sandal maker. However, Jack has found a new career. The aptitude he demonstrates for raising money soon brings him clients eager to benefit from that ability. Before long, Jack is running thirty-seven arts organizations. The remainder of the story follows Jack's adventures as an arts administrator. Keillor generates humor from both the absurdities of some of the artistic ideas and the treatment of an aesthetic subject in the style of hard-boiled detective fiction.

"Don: The True Story of a Young Person" was written during a time when punk rock bands were making news across America because of their on-stage antics. Particularly shocking were the exploits of one performer who was said to eat live chickens on stage. In this story, Don, the protagonist, is a Midwestern teenager who lives with his parents, goes to school, and plays in a band called Trash. That in itself is enough to worry Don's parents. Trash sings lyrics such as

> I'm gonna ride my mower all
>   around this town
> Cut everybody who's been trying to
>   put me down! (33–34)

In the course of playing at the President's Day County 4-H Poultry Show, one member of Trash gets carried away and bites a chicken. The chicken is checked out by a veterinarian and will be just fine, but the community is now up in arms. Eventually, through a series of incidents both ludicrous and poignant, Trash makes it big even though by that time Don's heart is no longer in the music or the performance.

Four of the pieces in Part One relate to radio station WLT. The characters are composites of personalities familiar to listeners of early radio, particularly of local rather than syndicated shows. In "WLT (The Edgar Era)," brothers Roy and Edgar Elmore begin broadcasting from their restaurant in order to advertise. Their restaurant, which serves six sandwiches, is successful, but it is not frequented by "better" families, who consider sandwiches food for the lower classes. Edgar longs for more genteel patronage. When hiring a string quartet and writing sophisticated ads fail to bring the elite, Roy suggests a radio broadcast that will take the restaurant "right *to* the Pillsburys in their own homes" (45). That is the beginning of station WLT. Its call letters stand for "With Lettuce and Tomato."

"The Slim Graves Show" is about Slim Graves and his wife Billie Ann. They have an early morning singing show on WLT. When Billie Ann becomes romantically involved with another of the show's singers, Courteous Carl, she must choose between Slim and Carl. She does this with the help of the listeners, who vote by buying boxes of SunRise Waffles with either Slim's picture or Carl's picture on the box, depending on whom they think Billie Ann should choose. Keillor uses the narrative voice of a fan to tell this tale. His accurate grasp of the fan's point of view makes this one of the most effective stories in the collection.

Walter "Dad" Benson's story is told in "Friendly Neighbor." Dad spent many years on WLT playing the part of Dad Benson, a down-to-earth philosopher who dispensed gentle advice through the show "Friendly Neighbor." A noontime program, it consisted of Dad, his daughter Jo, and her husband Frank. They chatted, gave the livestock report, and told stories. Sometimes they listened to an imaginary radio program, "The Muellers." The show within a show was created as a vehicle for giving the advice people wrote in for without embarrassing those who had written. The Muellers would face a certain situation on their "show," and Dad would comment on it on "Friendly Neighbor." That worked very well until Dad got a letter from a little girl whose father had abandoned the family for another woman. When the situation was dramatized by the Muellers, Dad disapproved of the father's deed. Nevertheless, many listeners wrote in to protest that the subject was too explicit for radio. In face of such criticism, Dad retired. Almost every year since then, his friends and relatives have held a dinner to honor him and promote better relations between rivals North Dakota, and Minnesota, both states where Dad once lived. Dad hoped to make the states friendly neighbors.

The final radio piece is "The Tip-Top Club." Keillor tells how the club began through a suggestion by a fan and is made up of WLT listeners who call in to the announcer, Bud Swenson, to give household hints and to talk about their children, pets, vacations, gardens, health, and the weather. Controversy is not allowed, so religion and politics are off limits. In order to ensure that no controversial subject is introduced, Alice the switchboard girl screens the calls, and Harlan the engineer stands by ready to cut off any speaker who shows a tendency to break the rules. The only way to get the telephone number of the show is from another Tip-Topper, as the listeners are called, thus eliminating most of the people who might not want to observe the restrictions. Things begin to fall apart when Bud retires and a new announcer, Wayne Bargy, takes over. Wayne is divorced, has no children, and lives in an apartment, so he has little interest in the subjects usually discussed by the Tip-Toppers. Instead, he wants to talk about his divorce, therapy, traveling, movies, and dining out. The Tip-Toppers love to hate Wayne, until his show is changed to a rock format and Wayne is replaced by another announcer who never gives his name on the air.

"Jack Schmidt on the Burning Sands" takes the reader back to the detective turned arts administrator. In this story Jack faces difficulties when Roland Smollett, a member of his board of directors, decides to put his nephew in Jack's job. Jack becomes a freelance writer of grant proposals. He knows how to put in the magic words that produce success with granting institutions. He also knows how to be specific enough to make a potential donor think he can be a leader in the arts but "not so clear as to give him an excuse to quibble over details" (92). The story is a spoof of proposal writing as well as the quirks of donors.

Keillor often writes from the viewpoints of characters into whose personalities he slips with a comfortable familiarity. In "My North Dakota Railroad Days," the narrator is an unnamed former employee of the North Dakota State Railroad. He laments the wreck of a once proud train known as the Prairie Queen and the dishonesty that caused the crash along with the loss of the employees' pension fund and club house. Because of the crooked dealing of various people connected with the railroad, the Prairie Queen jumped the tracks into the Red River, where on a quiet day her bell is still heard being tolled by the current.

Part Two addresses issues of baseball. "Attitude" deals with the ideal state of mind with which to play pickup games. For the first time in his life, the speaker is taking his game seriously. It is not the brainless plays he minds, but the attitude of his teammates. He thinks each player should at least pretend to be sorry for his mistakes. Doing so gives the others on the team the opportunity to reassure him that his mistake was no big deal, and the game can continue being played with some dignity. Proper attitudes can be created using various techniques, such as approaching the batter's box appropriately or spitting frequently. Style is "what it's all about" (123). The speaker details six things that Big Leaguers do. He contends that doing the same in Slow Pitch shows the correct attitude.

In the next piece, a note advises that Bill Horne is sick today, so his column, "Around the Horne by Bill Horne," has been written by Ed Farr. Presented as an actual newspaper column, the article describes a minor league baseball team with a very poor record. Farr is the new manager who is attempting to rejuvenate the team by using psychoanalysis. Relying heavily on psychological jargon, Farr examines the reasons the team is doing so badly. The first thing he blames is the fans themselves; he feels the team only needs self-confidence in order to win, and the fans have not been patient enough for that to happen. Now the team is not sure if it is possible to win at all. Farr believes if the fans get to know the players better it will create a "helpful partnership for dynamic change" (125). That is his purpose in writing the column. He analyzes the problems of the various positions, from the pitchers with pitcher's block to the catcher who feels his manhood is threatened by hard pitches. Farr pleads with the fans to notice the good qualities of the players rather than always concentrating on their faults.

"The New Baseball" is another look at what might be called the "psychologizing" of the game. Because of changes in the perception of the human condition brought about by writers such as Camus and Sartre, players have changed from approaching the plate determined to give the ball a mighty swat to simply experiencing "at-batness." The analytical narrator comments, "In contemporary baseball, they agree, cause-and-effect sequentiality is giving way to simple concurrence of phenomena as the crisis in baseball's system of linear reaction brings on a new 'system' of concentric and reflexive responses, and the old stately inwardness of the game is losing out to, or giving in to, outwardness, or rather awayness" (131). Although in the past great pitchers and hitters were praised because of craft, now baseball fans will see the merit in the "static balance" of baseball and will cheer the "natural organic unity" (131) of a game in which no one scores. Keillor continues in this manner throughout the piece, making fun of the pop psychology that was all the rage in the 1970s.

Keillor creates a narrator who mocks himself in "How Are the Legs, Sam?" Legs are his big problem in playing baseball even though he has not played a game since high school. He thinks of Sam, a player who is beginning to feel the strain of age after fifteen years in the majors. People keep telling Sam he is looking good, but his manager has offered him a job as a scout. The narrator says he himself should get into shape; maybe this winter he can begin running and get his legs ready for a game in the spring.

Part Three is almost exclusively topical, addressing current events and trends. As such, the reader needs some familiarity with what was going on when the pieces were written in order to fully appreciate their meaning. For those who lack familiarity, the material itself can serve as an often hilarious explanation of what occurred in the public life of America in the thirteen years covered by the mostly satirical articles.

"The New Washington: An Inside Story" is first, although if the pieces were arranged chronologically, it would be last. The basis of the article is a comment made by Charles Wick, a member of President Ronald Reagan's "Kitchen Cabinet." According to Wick, people suffering from the slow economy liked hearing about the privileged life of Washington insiders just as people in the Depression enjoyed seeing movies about the wealthy. The story is written as if Washington were Hollywood. Tour buses go by the homes of politicians, and tour guides who attend government night school are just waiting for their big break. There is even a suicide attempt from the large letters that spell out "WASHINGTON" on a hillside.

"U.S. Still on Top, Says Rest of World" begins with a statement by President Richard Nixon that "America today is Number One in the world" (150). The piece is written as though there were an Association of World Leaders who cast their votes in various categories, such as Best Credo and Most Telephones. The article mocks American smugness as well as popular surveys. The conclusion pretends to be sobering: although the United States has won the number one spot forty-five times, it still trails the Roman Empire, the British Empire, and the Mongol Horde in total wins.

The ninety-third Congress is seeking a way, in "Congress in Crisis: The Proximity Bill," to prevent constituents from bumping, tugging, and otherwise manhandling their congressional representatives. In this piece Keillor shows that the executive branch of government is not the only target of his pen. Legislators are equally qualified.

The remainder of the pieces in Part Three cover a variety of subjects, all topical. Two spoof the human tendency to judge quality by something easily quantified. "Re: The Tower Project" is Keillor's reaction to the construction of the Sears Tower in Chicago. It makes fun of those who find merit in the ability to construct the world's tallest building while "How It Was in America a Week Ago Tuesday" is his response to "bean counters," those who raise the mundane to new heights by counting things. The popular magazines that actually publish such articles are the real object of his mockery here.

Even action comics are open to parody in "Mission to Mandala," where Joe and Jim battle Celanese terrorists on the island of Mandala. Although trapped in a mine shaft and operating under radio silence that prevents them from contacting their ship, the two enterprising members of the First Brigade manage to escape by an underground river. In *Don Quixote*, Cervantes mocks the then popular practice of digressing in the middle of exciting adventures to tell how the author came across the story. In similar vein, Keillor mocks the interruptions caused by comic book fan letters. In an exaggeration of the disruption they cause, he has one letter point out that, according to *Jane's Guns*, the Celanese SM-82s should go "RA-A-A-AT-RAA-A-A-A-AT" rather than "BLAM-BLAAAMMM" as shown in the comic.

The section concludes with "Nana Hami Ba Reba," a burlesque of science fiction and the United States' unsuccessful attempt to convert to the metric system. Here metrification includes language and reflects the agonies suffered by the main character, a la *1984* and *Brave New World*.

Most of Part Four is also topical. In 1977 Nancy Friday wrote a popular book entitled *My Mother, Myself*. Keillor's parody is called "My Stepmother, Myself." In the manner of women's magazine articles, he reports interviews with "Snow," "Gretel," and "Cinderella," who now contend that there were understandable reasons for the atrocious acts perpetrated by their stepmothers. Snow admits she was not supportive enough of the Queen; Gretel claims her stepmother was simply offering her independence at an early age; Cinderella appreciates the fact that her stepmother treats her as an ordinary person rather than a royal.

"Plainfolks" takes a wildly exaggerated look at a set of publications, the *Foxfire* books. Starting with magazine articles in 1968 and eventually resulting in several volumes of collected folklore, the *Foxfire* series attempted to preserve the pioneer skills of America. The pioneer skills the Keillor lampoon attempts to preserve include customizing cars and building cinder block bookcases.

The antiestablishment attitude of the 1960s and 1970s was expressed in the espousal of various causes, such as civil rights and world peace, and in sometimes antithetical movements. Young people longing for independence defiantly urged one another, "Do your own thing." Yet at the same time they banded together in communes to experience a return to nature, the past, and a simpler life. Those who lacked the temerity to leave jobs and family could have a less complete communal experience by belonging to a cooperative, a type of venture frequently formed in the sixties and seventies in an effort to provide inexpensive household needs. "The People's Shopper" is Keillor's version of a flyer sent out by a coop. Shoppers can choose from such purveyors as The Whole Wheat Food Co-op, The Phantom Stomach Alternative Cafe, or St. Paul's Episcopal Drop-In Hair Center.

"Your Wedding and You" spoofs promotional brochures. It is from the 100 Flowers Bridal Shop and gives extensive information on the new types of wedding ceremonies that became popular in the 1970s when brides and grooms started writing their own vows in attempts to be distinctive. The brochure advises its readers not to reject "traditional" weddings of white tunics, songs by Peter, Paul, and Mary, and daisy crowns just to be different. But if, after careful thought, they should choose an Alternative Wedding, it should reflect their own personalities. One couple given as an example said their vows while chained to the gate of an industrial polluter.

There were so many causes being brought to public attention in the 1970s that Keillor felt the time was right to take up his own cause: shy rights. In "Shy Rights: Why Not Pretty Soon?" he calls the discrimination against shys a major disgrace. Shys rarely speak up for themselves. Nevertheless, they need to formulate a plan and have a slogan in case they ever do decide to make any demands.

The narrator of "The Lowliest Bush a Purple Sage Would Be" accompanies a poet as he listens to nature. The poet may sit for hours staring at a tree, which he may finally understand is his mother. During the visit narrator and poet sit by a frozen lake and listen to walleye fish under the ice singing songs in deep baritone voices. Nature takes a long time to speak—a tree may take a week to say one sentence—and poets are really the only ones who will take the time to listen. However, it can be an annoyance to be continually accosted by squirrels and birds wanting to express their opinions.

Mr. and Mrs. Robert Shepard hire a live-in prostitute for their sixteen-year-old in "Local Family Keeps Son Happy." They see more of him and no longer have to worry about his being out late in the car. The story is presented as a news article. The ironic contrast between the unusual material and the matter-of-fact reporting provides the humor.

"Oya Life These Days" is an amusing look at the Oyas, a sociological oddity whose main feature seems to be the ability to irritate others, while "Your Transit Company" is another spoof of promotional brochures. This one supposedly originates with a city's transit authority. In an attempt to convince riders that city buses are no longer just dependable but boring transportation, the brochure promotes exciting new alternatives. Drivers' uniforms are color-coordinated with the buses in vivid shades of primary colors. Passengers may choose from a variety of theme buses, including the Senior Bus, the Teen Bus, the Star Wars Bus, and the Disco Bus. Best of all is the Freedom Bus, which is randomly selected by the company. Instead of going to work or to the dentist, riders on the Freedom Bus find after they board that they will be taken for a day of fun, perhaps to a ball game or to the driver's house for lunch and a swim.

"Be Careful" warns readers that danger can be found when and where they least expect it, a fact Americans were reminded of by the breakup of the Skylab space station in the 1970s. The pieces fell harmlessly into the ocean, but at the time there was uncertainty about where they would come to earth. In an exaggeration of articles on safety, Keillor lists rules such as "Stay with the group" and "Watch where you're going." However, he knows readers are probably reading this article in poor light even though they know better.

In "Ten Stories for Mr. Richard Brautigan and Other Stories" Keillor casts a wry glance at another author's works by offering his own similar stories, beginning with one that is only one sentence in length. Brautigan was a poet who became part of the Beat Generation of the 1950s but whose greatest popularity came during the 1960s. His work, which centered on his personal life and daily experiences, Keillor finds very easy to parody.

Part Five deals with more serious subjects and includes two articles that are largely autobiographical. Because Keillor uses many different narrative voices in the previous pieces, his own voice comes as a surprise here. In an interview he admitted that articles based on personal experience were easier for him to write than those in which he labored to find the right combination of voice, tone, and diction. These two pieces, "After a Fall" and "Drowning 1954," needed almost no revision. He explained, "There are a few stories that I have written that are like that, and I'm grateful for every one" (Schumacher 35).

In the first piece, "After a Fall," Keillor muses about a fall that occurred for no reason he could determine. He simply went out the door one day and fell down his front steps. A jogger stopped to ask if he was all right, then smiled slightly and ran on when he told her he was fine. But he was not fine, and Keillor wishes she had helped him up and sat with him a few moments. Her smile told him that, although she was too polite to give in to the urge, she had wanted to laugh.

With chagrin, he remembers once laughing when his son tripped. At the time he dismissed his son's anger by saying, "Oh, don't be so sensitive" (253). Now Keillor realizes that he was at fault: it was not funny and he was being insensitive. He recalls other falls, in some of which he narrowly escaped serious injury. He gives them humorous names but the potential danger underlying each gives the humor an edge. He is particularly grateful that his fall off a ladder did not injure his small son, who was watching from below.

He recalls a fall when he was nineteen and undertook his "first venture as a naked person" (259). Donna, a friend whose fundamentalist upbringing had been similar to his own, invited him and four others to her father's sauna when her parents were away from home. Careful to avoid looking at each other's nudity, the pseudosophisticates were doing well at being "natural and free" (259) until a cold shower nozzle went wild. Panicked as much by guilt as by the shock of the water, they fell while diving for their clothes. Now twenty years later Keillor wants to reassure Donna that God did not turn on the cold water to punish her.

There is little humor in "A Drunkard's Sunday." In this story a host drinks too much at his own afternoon party. Suddenly ashamed of his behavior, he exits the gathering, choosing to cry alone in the woods until his guests have gone. He moves from maudlin fear to remorse to grandiose plans for a new life, all of which fade away by the end. Sadly the reader feels the drunkard will have other such Sundays.

"Happy to Be Here," published originally in the *New Yorker* as "Found Paradise," again pokes fun at the 1970s counterculture and its search for happiness by returning to nature. Keillor uses elements of personal experience in describing a move to a farm. He can laugh at himself as the budding writer/narrator who sees everything, including his morning shower, in terms of how it will read in print. Nevertheless, the narrative voice is not his own but one of an idealistic artist who, in imitation of Thoreau, finds paradise in the simple life and concludes that he is "happy to be here" (271).

In "Drowning 1954" Keillor recalls the summer when his mother sent him to the YMCA in Minneapolis for swimming lessons. Finding that he hated the instructor and was afraid of the water, he tried to drop the lessons. But his mother was frightened by his cousin's drowning and insisted Keillor learn to swim. Consequently, he pretended to continue the lessons. In reality he found things to do around Minneapolis instead. He went to the public library and to radio station WCCO for the "Good Neighbor Time" show. As fascinated as he was by the radio activity, he was terrified that he would be interviewed on the air and his shameful secret would come out. He was convinced his deceit was the first step toward becoming a bum like those he saw on the street. He says, "I still remember the sadness of wandering in downtown Minneapolis in 1954, wasting my life and losing my soul, and my great relief when the class term ended and I became a kid again" (275). Eventually Keillor learned to swim, but now he feels great tenderness as he watches his own son, a seven-year-old, gathering up courage to go into the water.

Keillor could have ended the collection with "Happy to Be Here," from which he took the book title. Instead the final piece is one that looks back to his own youth and forward to the future of his son. In that way he ties together the disparate articles in the collection and reminds the reader of the universality in human experience.

CHARACTER DEVELOPMENT

Characterization is a crucial element of fiction. Plot can engage the reader, but characterization is what keeps most readers interested. As readers get to know fictional characters, they begin to care about what happens to them. This is particularly true if the characters are round as opposed to flat. Flat characters tend to be one-dimensional. They are often stereotypes who exhibit one strong trait, such as jealousy or bravery. Round characters, on the other hand, demonstrate many character traits. Like many people, complex characters sometimes display contradictory traits.

In a novel or a long short story, a writer can develop character thoroughly. In addition to revealing character by what someone does or says, the skillful writer may show discrepancies—between a character's words and actions or between the character's actions and the way that same character is perceived by others. Such complexity takes time to develop—time the short story writer seldom has.

Because many of the pieces in *Happy to Be Here* are parodies, satirical commentaries, or brief humorous writings in which character is incidental to the fun-poking, characters tend to be flat. Nevertheless, there are

GARDNER HARVEY LIBRARY
Miami University-Middletown
Middletown, Ohio 45042

a few characters complex enough to be analyzed, and Jack Schmidt is one. Jack's speech patterns and libidinous attitude toward Bobbie Jo, his secretary, are part of the hard-boiled detective stereotype that Keillor is spoofing. However, there is more to Jack than stereotype. Ollie, the elevator boy, says Jack represents "the spirit of inquiry, the scientific mind, eighteenth-century enlightenment" (19). The Enlightenment, like the Renaissance, prized versatility. Jack's versatility may come from necessity, but he demonstrates the ability to excel in several different arenas. As a professional sleuth, he mingled with bookies; now he attends arts conferences in Rio and Nassau and meets with the mother of a mining heir. His imagination enables him to combine arts projects with the donors most apt to fund them, to turn kooky ideas into going concerns. Even the Minnesota Anti-Dance Ensemble, whose members picket the corporations that give it money, is not too weird for Jack. He admits, "I have met weirder on the street" (20). Unlike the typical arts manager, who makes small talk at lawn parties, Jack uses his street savvy to ask for the impossible sums that guarantee success for his organizations.

In addition, Jack is resilient in the face of adversity. He faces one setback after another and always manages to turn negatives into positives. When the highway department takes the Twin City Arts Mall, he figures out how to convert a problem highway median into an Arts Highway. When he loses his job to a board member's nephew, he does not give up. He simply works another angle, eventually triumphing. Were this not humor, the reader would be completely caught up in Jack's struggles to survive. As it is, the reader knows Jack will come out on top, but that knowledge does not diminish the admiration for his indomitable spirit.

Another complex character is the drunkard in "The Drunkard's Sunday." Keillor tells the story as a third-person narration primarily limited to the drunkard's thoughts. As the protagonist weaves through his party guests, he condemns them for drinking while neglecting their children although he is guilty of doing the same thing. This attitude is less hypocrisy than a reluctance to face reality. Recognition of his own neglect reduces him to tears and causes him to abandon his guests. In imagination he foresees family tragedies, all a result of his drinking. The phantasms might be attributed to his alcoholic state if his sober fantasies were not just as exaggerated. He dreams of providing his family with all the wonderful things of life; he imagines energetically tackling all the projects he has let slide. He vows he will never overindulge again. He will "set things straight" (264).

The drunkard's alcohol problem seems rooted in his avoidance of reality. That avoidance causes the ambivalence he has toward his drinking. Like an adolescent excusing behavior because "everyone does it," he recalls movie scenes in which heavy drinking seemed to impair no one. Yet almost as soon as he thinks of the movies, he is filled with self-recrimination and pledges never to drink again. The reader cannot take such pledges seriously. As the drunkard dreams of what he will do in the future, the present slips away. By the end he is alone again, this time with pain that seems a physical manifestation of his mental and spiritual anguish.

The imitation brochures, pretend pamphlets, and fake news columns contain no characters at all. However, these two examples give evidence that Keillor can create character complexity when it is necessary and appropriate.

THEMATIC ISSUES

Reviewer Keith Mano points out that most of the pieces in *Happy to Be Here* are parodies, not satires. Although both the satirist and the parodist overstate, Mano distinguishes between the two by reminding the reader of the purpose of the satirist, that is, to bring about improvement by pointing out the errors of institutions or humankind. Keillor, he says, writes without anger. He has no "righteous underfur."

As a humorist, Keillor's purpose is to provoke laughter. The fun he provides is an end in itself. As he makes the reader laugh, however, he poses serious questions and introduces serious themes. Most of Keillor's themes pertain to the realization that happiness is based on familiar virtues, one of which is love. Love finds various expressions in his writings and is perhaps the most prevalent theme that he addresses. The traditional divisions of erotic love, familial love, and brotherly love can all be found in *Happy to Be Here*. Erotic love causes the problems in "The Slim Graves Show." In the story of Don Beeman, familial love is stretched to its limits during Don's growing independence from his parents while "The Drunkard's Sunday" speaks movingly of a father's protective love of his wife and daughter and his perceived failure of that love. "My North Dakota Railroad Days" tells of love of a brotherhood that has been wronged by powerful people.

In these situations, one sees the anxiety and anger that can result when one person's idea of love fails to meet the expectations of another person or when the loved one suffers at the hands of others. However, love in all its permutations and with all its imperfections, is preferable to any other emotion. Keillor seems to say that it is all one has, and thus it should be safeguarded to the best of one's ability.

Tolerance, another virtue, can be considered an ancillary to love because it is love that makes tolerance possible. In every piece in *Happy to Be Here* there is some form of tolerance. Keillor has the gift of being able to include himself in much of his satire so that the reader takes little or no offense at it. That ability is a measure of tolerance and is one reason that this particular theme recurs so often in Keillor's writings. The effects of the lack of tolerance are seen in the story of Don Beeman, where an entire community overreacts. People do not examine the situation from a broad enough perspective to allow for the reconciliation of mistakes and misunderstandings. The baseball stories in Part Two, as humorous as they are, call quite openly for tolerance and remind readers that no one is exempt from the burdens of aging and self-doubt. "How Are the Legs, Sam?" acknowledges that most people mean well, but often do not act on their good intentions. Win or lose, all are human, doing the best they can in what are often trying circumstances.

In such pieces as "My North Dakota Railroad Days" and "Drowning 1954," Keillor concentrates on the uncertainty and anguish that can result when life deals harsh blows. However, these difficulties can be accepted with fortitude, another virtue, while in the autobiographical pieces, Keillor expresses gratitude for small pleasures. He is thankful that his life has gone as well as it has. He makes the reader think about his or her own blessings and rejoice. Love, tolerance, fortitude, and gratitude—all are homely treasures, but Keillor is able to convince the reader of their value.

ALTERNATE READING: FREUDIAN CRITICISM

Although critical analysis of literature has a history extending as far back as Aristotle, many forms of contemporary criticism are quite recent in origin. One form, psychoanalytical criticism, is primarily based on the works of Sigmund Freud (1856–1939). Even though there are other psychological approaches, from Jung to Maslow to Lesser, those approaches have grown from expansions, modifications, or rejections of Freud's original psychoanalytical theories.

According to Freud, "the division of mental life into what is conscious and what is unconscious is the fundamental premise on which psychoanalysis is based" (Freud, *Ego* 697). The conscious and unconscious govern the behavior of every human being. Freud believed that very little behavior originates in the conscious realm of thought and that by far the greater part of behavior plays itself out in the unconscious. He likened the mind to an iceberg with the unconscious being the large percentage below the surface (MacHovec 14).

Freud theorized that the human personality can be divided into three realms: the id, the ego, and the superego. The id is totally unconscious and is focused on the pleasure principle. The id's goal is the avoidance of pain and the fulfillment of its desire for pleasure, including but not limited to sex. This desire may be for pleasure that is acceptable in moderation but unacceptable when pursued to the exclusion of all else. Because repression of the id is necessary for people to conduct themselves in society, the functions of the id are unknown to people themselves. However, the id strongly influences behavior and methods of thinking (Hall 22–27).

When people enter a social milieu, the ego comes into play. "Instead of the pleasure principle the ego is governed by the reality principle" (Hall 28). Operating in both the conscious and the unconscious, the ego is aware from experience that cooperation with others is necessary for successful existence and that the pursuit of pleasure above all else can be counterproductive, even disastrous. Consequently, it works at compromise between the id and the superego (MacHovec 32).

The super ego is what many call the conscience. It stems from the restraints placed on every human being by parents, teachers, and institutions in order to maintain the social order. This super ego is what governs the repressed functions of the id, but it is not truly a part of most people's concept of self. It is simply something that has been imposed, usually from earliest childhood (Hall 31).

As unlikely as it may seem, a psychoanalytical reading of "Mission from Mandala" can be enlightening. Joe and Jim, the Able Baker Comics heroes, are trapped in a mine shaft surrounded by Celanese terrorists. Although Joe and Jim are under radio silence, they manage to tap out a message to their ship standing out at sea. However, when they escape by swimming an underground river, they mistakenly head away from the ship in shark-infested waters while their captain is unaware of their danger. As Captain O'Connor paces the deck of the ship, waiting, Nurse Nancy watches him and wonders how she can tell him that he has an aneurysm as large as a fist.

Joe and Jim here represent the repressed id, safely buried deep in a mine shaft and out of conscious contact. The id feels besieged by impediments to the fulfillment of its desire, in this case by the Celanese, who symbolize the ego. The ego unconsciously knows that in order for the person to survive, the id must be constantly repressed. Even though the id attempts to emerge from repression in the tapped-out message to the ship, an escape will result in death or severe injury, either physical or psychological. Exactly that occurs when Joe and Jim find their way out of the mine shaft. The id has escaped and subsequently finds itself surrounded by mortal danger as symbolized by the sharks.

Pacing the deck of the ship is the super ego in the guise of Captain O'Connor. He represents the accumulation of authoritative training that has been brought to bear on the id and the ego. Watching over these two aspects of personality with a vigilance that assures their well-being, the super ego is nevertheless in danger itself. This danger takes the form of an aneurysm, another representation of the id, that may wreak havoc at any moment should it break from repression. However, in spite of the danger, the super ego constantly plans for the safety of the id and the ego, never allowing itself to admit defeat.

One of the most widely known of Freud's theories is that of the Oedipus complex. Named for the mythical Greek king who unwittingly killed his father and married his mother, the complex is manifested in males, who have sexual feelings toward their mothers and view their fathers as rivals. Because these desires of the id are unacceptable, a son who is not psychoneurotic represses them and turns to other, acceptable sources of fulfillment (Freud, *Interpretation* 246–47).

A good example of Oedipal repression can be found in Don Beeman, the teenager who becomes a "geek" rocker in "Don: The True Story of a Young Person." Don clearly is attempting to break away from his parents, particularly his mother. The turning point in his decision about whether to remain with his band is amplified by the words of one of the band's new songs:

> All my life you told me "Shut
>   up and behave."
> Well, from now on, Mama, your
>   boy's gonna scream and rave.
> I know you hate to see me playing
>   rock and roll,
> But Mom, I gotta break your
>   heart to save my soul. (37–38)

Don knows, both consciously and unconsciously, that he cannot remain within the sphere of his mother's influence. What he does not know is why. He has repressed the desire of the id for the murder of his father and marriage to his mother. These are unacceptable desires, to which he cannot allow conscious thought or action, else disaster will follow. The alternative is what Don arrives at in conscious thought through the ego and super ego: he must leave both his parents.

Psychoanalytical theorists often conclude that characters reveal much about the author who created them. This seems unlikely with the Joe and Jim spoof of a comic but very plausible with Don Beeman. Keillor projects his own youthful predicament onto the young rock musician. Keillor's own outlet was writing, not music, but for both Keillor and Don parental attempts to stifle creative activity can be equated with attempts to squelch rising sexuality and the rivalry it will produce. According to Freud's theory, this is the dilemma faced by every son. Both Keillor and Don successfully escape their parents, thus avoiding the tragedy that awaits failure to do so.

A Freudian look at *Happy to Be Here* would be incomplete without also considering why the book appeals to readers. Those who enjoy humor at the expense of Washington power brokers may do so because they unconsciously wish to be in their place. In fact, the repressed wishes of many readers account for what they read about—the action of adventurers, the defiance of the counterculture, the missteps of youths. However, even that choice is too revealing for some people. They fear others will recognize that these are activities they would really like to do. Thus when they read about such subjects under the guise of humor, they provide a double layer of protection between the unconscious and the conscious mind. They can easily convince themselves that they are reading them only for fun.

4

Lake Wobegon Days
(1985)

Keillor's *Happy to Be Here* is a compilation of short stories and humorous pieces, most of which had appeared in print before its publication, but except for a prepublication excerpt in the *Atlantic*, the material in *Lake Wobegon Days* had not previously been published. That did not mean it was all new material, however. Keillor had told many of the stories as monologues on *A Prairie Home Companion*, and several were included in a set of tapes that went on sale in 1983. The four tapes, collectively entitled *News from Lake Wobegon*, were individually named for the seasons. The seasons serve as some of the divisions of the book as well.

On the morning radio show that eventually became *A Prairie Home Companion*, Keillor developed the format that brought him so much success on his later evening show. Lake Wobegon, however, was not part of that initial format. He first claimed as his hometown Freeport, where he was then living, or Brooklyn Park, where he grew up. One of his fictitious sponsors was Jack's Auto Repair. When listeners started to send in pictures of real shops with that name, he decided he needed to create a fictional setting for his stories. The result was Lake Wobegon (Radel B9). In explaining his choice of the name, he told one interviewer: "To me it sounded vaguely like an Indian word, so I could use it and also get some of the English meaning of the word—you know, 'bedraggled'— and still claim that it meant something else" (Damsker E12). When the evening version of *A Prairie Home Companion* began in 1974, Lake Wobegon was part of it. Gradually Keillor expanded the town and its inhabitants until the businesses, the residents, and their habits were all familiar to his listeners. In *Lake Wobegon Days* he translates that radio world into print.

Like a traditional epic or tale, the book has a distinctly oral flavor. The reader can almost hear the voice of the storyteller. However, *Lake Wobegon Days* is not a transcription of material first presented on the radio and then on tape. Instead it is a reworking of familiar material, a blending of new material with old. For instance, the written version of one monologue may be an expansion of the original. Another may be a condensation. In still another, such as the one about a refuge for children during a snowstorm, the story is basically the same, but Keillor changes the names. In addition, the material does not become static once it reaches print. Keillor told the story of "Tomato Butt" in a monologue that was part of the first set of tapes. That story appears here in the chapter entitled "Summer" with only slight modification. However, ten years later on a November 11, 1995, broadcast, he referred again to Tomato Butt without telling the entire story.

Keillor begins *Lake Wobegon Days* with history. A footnote on the first page details the town of Lake Wobegon according to the Federal Writers Project, and a quote from another supposed source makes the history seem authentic. Keillor even explains why the town cannot be found on any map: incompetent surveyors are to blame. The town may be fictional, but what is not fictional are the incidents of small town life. From the boy jumping on the garage bell hose on page two to the fear of putting one's tongue on a frozen pump handle on page 246, the details ring true to everyone who has experienced rural America.

Although Keillor uses a first-person narrator in this book as he does in his monologues, the identity of that narrator is not always clear beyond the fact that he is or has been part of the Lake Wobegon community. Sometimes the narrator refers to himself as Gary Keillor and his stories are highly autobiographical, but at other times it is clear that both the narrator and the story are as invented as the town.

The book is divided into groups of tales loosely organized around central themes. In some sections the connection seems tenuous, made by free association, but usually Keillor manages to tie things together by the end. The strength of the tales lies in their humor, their evocation of shared memories, and their recognition of universal truths.

PLOT DEVELOPMENT

Plot depends on conflict. The normal plot outline of a short story depicts an exposition, a complication based on the conflict, a turning point, and a resolution. Few of the stories in this book follow the standard outline, however. Partly that is due to the fact that many are not short stories in the strict sense of the word. Some resemble folk tales while others are more like village gossip or commentary. One story segues into a second that blends with a third. Some explore character; others relate amusing incidents; still others reflect on uncomfortable realities most people would like to ignore. All use the Lake Wobegon setting as background.

The first section of the book is entitled "Home." After the supposed history and geography, Keillor gives a short introduction to the town of Lake Wobegon, the county seat of Mist County. He explains that its name comes "from an Indian phrase that means either 'Here we are!' or 'we sat all day in the rain waiting for [you]' " (8). Like Thornton Wilder's *Our Town*, which begins with a birth and ends with death, "Home" discusses both those extremes of human existence. The rest of the section is a combination of stages in between. Many memories of the narrator—a conversation about creation when he was four, a fight about predestination when he was an adolescent, and the recollection of singing "Tell Me Why"—revolve around the nature of God. Other memories establish recognition in readers by recounting experiences most have undergone: young love, attempts to remake self, bluster camouflaging insecurity. Much of Keillor's humor in those passages comes from the ability of readers to recall similar actions of their own, actions that now seem amusing.

In the second chapter, "New Albion," Keillor returns to telling history. After the early explorers, he reports, the first settlers were Unitarian missionaries who came to "convert the Indians to Christianity by the means of interpretive dance" (25). New Albion was the name they gave to their chosen site on what the French called Lac Malheur [Lake Unhappiness]. This chapter comes closer to short story form than most of the others. It follows one of the purported settlers, Henry Francis Watt, from the founding of the town and New Albion College through the boom period of the new community to the bust period that follows. Watt struggles with conflict from an outside manipulator, from the weather, and from his own flaws. After he finishes Watt's story, Keillor moves on to tell of the first railroad, first primary school, first killing, and first doctor. By the end of the chapter, the town has become Lake Wobegon.

"Forebears" is the name of the third chapter. It tells of the first Norwegian settler, Magnus Oleson, who is revered by his descendants until they discover, from letters sent home to Norway, that he deserted from General George McClellan's army. That is embarrassing to some of the Daughters of the Pioneers who traced their Norwegian ancestry to him. In this passage Keillor pokes gentle fun at organizations that attempt to establish status through ancestors. Had the women not been vying for honor guard positions according to whose forefathers had arrived first, they would not have found out about Oleson's desertion. The chapter goes on to tell of the other forebears, such as the Tollefson party who mistakenly went to Dakota Territory in search of a great lake. Like Oleson, they created much of their own difficulty.

Recurrent characters in the monologues on *A Prairie Home Companion* are Norwegian bachelor farmers. Here Keillor introduces the first one of those, and he also tells of the first German settler, August Krebsbach from Bavaria. Although he ends with modern-day anecdotes, Keillor uses the chapter to establish the makeup of the community. Like many real Minnesota towns, Lake Wobegon is predominantly comprised of people of Norwegian or German heritage. This chapter gives the immigrant stories.

"Sumus quod sumus" is the motto on Lake Wobegon's town crest; it is also the title of the next chapter. It means "We are what we are" (6), and in this chapter Keillor explains what exactly that is. He points out what is special about the town. The Statue of the Unknown Norwegian is one thing. Another is the Lake Wobegon runestone. Although the runestone is ignored in a museum most of the year, it is taken to the school on Columbus Day so that school children can see that Eric the Red really did precede Columbus in the new world, a world that should have been named The United States of Erica. Keillor has great fun with the stone's inscription as he does with the description of Ralph's Pretty Good Grocery and other retail establishments in Lake Wobegon. Some residents may go to St. Cloud to buy a cheaper toaster or Calvin Klein eyeglasses, but most buy locally because they know the shopkeepers. Besides, as he points out, "Calvin Klein isn't going to come with the Rescue Squad and he isn't going to teach your children about redemption by grace" (96).

The chapter ends with a detailed story about Flag Day and a celebration organized by Herman Hochstetter, who runs a dry goods store.

Overstocked in red, white, and blue baseball caps, he thinks up a way to use them by creating a living flag. It is a great success the first year, and people are proud to be in the picture that is taken from the roof of a nearby building. However, human nature being what it is, in ensuing years the hundreds of participants become difficult. They want to see what they are creating. Obviously that poses problems since leaving to look at it destroys what they want to see. The attempts to resolve the problem complete the story and the chapter.

Longtime listeners to *A Prairie Home Companion* often assume that Keillor is Lutheran. The two religious groups about which he talks the most are the Lutherans, mostly of Norwegian descent, and the Catholics, mostly of German descent. The Lutherans attend Lake Wobegon Lutheran Church, where David Ingqvist is the minister, and the Catholics attend Our Lady of Perpetual Responsibility, where Father Emil is priest. In the chapter entitled "Protestant," however, Keillor talks about the Sanctified Brethren, a fundamentalist sect that is similar to the Plymouth Brethren, the denomination of Keillor's parents. Because the Brethren were such a small group, Keillor claims no one had ever heard of them, and he found it easier to tell people he was Protestant. That comment provides the basis of the title.

This chapter is the most autobiographical in *Lake Wobegon Days*. The narrator details the worship services of the Sanctified Brethren as they gather in his aunt and uncle's living room. He attests to the quiet peace of the group as they wait for the Spirit to move someone to speak. Even as he observes the sweetness of the moment, however, he cannot mention it aloud because children, like women, are not supposed to speak in church.

Although they are already a small sect, the Brethren seem forever to split and splinter—over whether women should wear slacks, whether speaking in tongues is a desirable aim. Their fear of worldliness is borne out in an incident after the group starts going to St. Cloud for services. That excursion requires eating away from home, a new experience for the narrator's family. Keillor extracts humor from their leaving a restaurant after being asked whether they would like an alcoholic drink, but the embarrassment to the child narrator is acute. He admits badgering his parents about inconsistencies in their faith. Again there is recognizable humor here because the best of parents get caught in their inconsistencies by their bright children.

The narrator admits posing difficult questions about choices between the lesser of two evils. His father's answer to one of his posed dilemmas is to "wait until a Ford comes along" (112). That is the lead-in to the next part of the chapter, which begins, "In Lake Wobegon, car ownership is a matter of faith" (112). Lutherans, it seems, drive Fords purchased from the Bunsen Brothers, who are Lutherans, while Catholics drive Chevrolets bought from the Kruegers, who are Catholic. Because they are Protestant, the Brethren also drive Fords. However, not wishing to be taken for Lutherans, they attach to their license plates metal shields on which scripture verses are written in glass beads.

The narrative voice in this section is that of a teenage boy. Again there is recognition as he tells of unbolting the verses after leaving home and rebolting them before returning the family car. When he has a near accident, he takes a verse on Brother Louie's car as a warning. That leads into a sincere tribute to Louie. After earning an associate degree in night school, Louie sought employment in Minneapolis. On his first night there, however, he realized that his whole motivation came from worldly pride and he went back to Lake Wobegon. The ambivalence of the narrator in this section is similar to the ambivalence Keillor seems to have about his own fundamentalist upbringing. On the one hand, he admires the sincerity of convictions that his parents shared with other members of the Brethren, like Louie, but on the other, he was stifled by their attitudes toward the world, success in it, and what it takes to achieve that success.

There is a division in the middle of this chapter. As the Brethren see themselves as separated from the rest of the world, so the portion about them is separated from the rest of the chapter. Most of what follows the division is about ceremony. It begins with a Memorial Day celebration featuring both parade and performance. The traditional Catholic-Lutheran tension is found in the marchers and in the divided cemetery they march to. After mention of Queen Elizabeth's coronation comes the sad observation: "Life in a small town offered so little real ceremony" (124).

"Summer" comes next. August in Minnesota can be as hot as in the South. Anyone who doubts that will soon be disabused of the notion by this chapter. The inhabitants of Lake Wobegon try various activities as either escape or diversion from the stifling heat. Father Emil leaves for vacation during August, taking his annual trip to visit Civil War battlefields. Other people concentrate on their gardens and attempt to raise prize-winning produce. The narrator makes case after case for the purchase of an air conditioner, but Dad thinks air-conditioning is "for the weak and indolent" (132), a sign of decadence. Dad's opinion is not very different from that of most people in town. Those who do purchase air-conditioners seem to need an excuse. Hay fever and heat rash are accepted, but people are surprised when Mrs. Hoglund buys one because there is nothing wrong with her. The narrator comments, "If doing without makes you appreciate things more, I guessed the people of Lake Wobegon should be the happiest people in the world" (164).

"Summer" tells of Jack Krueger's failed attempt at founding a country club in Lake Wobegon. It purports to be for the purpose of playing golf, but Clarence Bunsen recognizes that it would be the first organization in town that was costly to join. He contends that if he wanted people to know he had money, he would not need to join a country club. He would just put the money on a stick and walk around town showing it off. Needless to say, the citizens of Lake Wobegon let the opportunity for such ostentation pass them by.

One of the most poignant stories is of Johnny Tollefson and his trip to St. Cloud to register for college. His mother, grandmother, aunt, and uncle are so proud of him that they all want to go along. Their presence causes intense embarrassment for Johnny, who wishes to appear suave and sophisticated when he arrives on campus. He contrasts his family to the Flambeaus, a fictional family in a mystery series that he has read and reread. The Flambeaus are everything his family is not. They live in a Manhattan apartment; they do exciting things on the spur of the moment; they treat their teenage son as an adult. The last point is particularly attractive to Johnny. He muses, "To call your parents by their first names, to sit around drinking fine wine with them—this never happens in Lake Wobegon!" (154).

True, Lake Wobegon is not filled with Nobel laureates like Emile Flambeau or former film stars like his wife Eileen. Instead it contains Norwegian bachelor farmers, some of whom are described in this chapter. Most of the people, however, are very ordinary—so ordinary, in fact, that they become quite recognizable to many readers who, like Keillor's uncles, may present themselves as all virtue to the young, yet giggle over their own youthful misdeeds when they think the young are not around. If they themselves have not had marital difficulties like the Dieners, they know someone who has. Likewise, they probably know someone who has had rheumatic fever like Muriel Krebsbach or abandoned family responsibility and disappeared like her father.

The next chapter, "School," tells of school experiences and elementary school teachers. Keillor fittingly finishes the account of a very jumpy teacher by giving questions for class discussion, one of which is "Do you think the author should have worked harder in school?" (174). Perhaps the answer should be "yes" because the rest of the chapter has less to do with school than it does with the activities of school-age children. One such activity is Scouting. The narrator's short-lived career as a Boy Scout results from his application of logic to semaphore practice. He cannot figure out its purpose. The reason given, that the Scouts can signal for help in case of a medical emergency, makes no sense when the Scoutmaster always has his car at the campsite. The thwarted Scoutmaster threatens to strip the Scouts of their badges as if they are actually in the army. The narrator, however, is impervious to such threats. He did not join the Scouts for the scouting part in the first place.

The chapter ends with several sports tales. The most interesting one tells of Wally Bunsen, who was nicknamed, "Old Hard Hands," because he could not afford a baseball glove and had learned to play without one. That distinction was the reason for both his rise to prominence and his fall from it. His is one of the more sobering stories that Keillor tells. Although Wally could turn privation into an asset, he could not adjust to a better situation. When he made it to the major leagues, the Cubs' requirement that he use a glove affected every aspect of his game, even his offense, and he lasted only one season. His eventual downfall follows the pattern of the traditional tragic hero and is just as sad.

In a town like Lake Wobegon, falls bring hunters, and the chapter called "Fall" is naturally going to contain hunting stories. The local lodge is not the Masons or Elks or Moose, but the Sons of Knute, who are portrayed here in a story about their memorial duck blind. Much of the chapter, however, is devoted to Thanksgiving, the most important fall holiday. Although many of Keillor's stories could take place in any small town across the United States, many are also site specific. Nowhere is this clearer than in the many instances when characters have to deal with Minnesota's weather.

"Over the river and through the woods" sing school children every November. They may never have seen a horse-drawn sleigh or be able to go to grandmother's house, but they are likely to participate in some kind of family gathering at Thanksgiving. Traveling today by auto, bus, or plane, they still go "home" for this popular holiday, and if they travel in Minnesota, they are apt to encounter the "white and drifted snow" of the song.

That is the experience of two families who attempt to visit Lake Wobegon. A blizzard that strikes the day before Thanksgiving makes movement difficult for those already there and almost impossible for those trying to reach the town. Christine Ingqvist, her husband, and children eventually get to St. Paul after hours spent in airports waiting for runways to be cleared. Once in St. Paul, they must spend the night in a hotel. As she shivers in her California raincoat, Christine looks out of a bus window at what seems like a scene from the Middle Ages with warmly dressed peasants struggling along the road.

On Thanksgiving morning she agonizes over whether they should attempt the drive to Lake Wobegon or wait until the next day. The streets in St. Paul are clear, but the weather announcer continues to warn against any unnecessary travel. Her dilemma is familiar to all who have listened to weather reports and tried to reconcile them with their own perceptions. Christine has told her parents they will not be able to travel until Friday. When she decides to go ahead and surprise her parents, it is fitting that their dinner turns out to be macaroni and cheese.

Barbara Bunsen and her husband Bill do not have the same difficulty in reaching Lake Wobegon. The concentration in her story is on her father Clarence and his disappointment when he thinks they will be unable to visit. When they do arrive, the focus shifts to the comfortable companionship of Barbara and her parents contrasted with the discomfort of her husband. The family members make so many references to people, places, and events Bill has never heard of that he decides the town is a cult to which he obviously does not belong.

Fall moves naturally into "Winter," the next chapter, and Thanksgiving merges into Christmas. The Christmas celebrations of a small town are seldom sophisticated, but they tend to be inclusive. Bud puts up the community decorations, and Ralph starts making *lutefisk*. The Catholic church presents a pageant, the Lutheran pastor prepares a sermon on what Christmas really means, and everyone goes caroling. From the church choirs and youth groups to the school choral groups and clubs, all participate, even the Sons of Knute although they sponsor the singing of Norwegian carols rather than singing them themselves.

Here the general description of Christmas activities mixes with personal stories of both childhood and adolescence. The child faces the familiar quandaries of trying to apportion eight dollars in savings to buy gifts for twelve people, of getting a long desired gift only to discover it has drawbacks. His parents express their own fears—his mother, that the tree will catch on fire and his father, that Christmas buying will leave him poor. The adolescent is depicted with more angst. He writes poems about a girl he admires but cannot bring himself to give them to her. Before a skiing date with a cousin of Chip Ingqvist, he practices kissing in case he should need to know how. As it turns out, he does.

Minnesota comes into its own in the winter, and Minnesotans, being used to the cold, enjoy the skating, skiing, and sledding that it affords. They revel in being able to withstand the accompanying hardships. Not so Lyle, a transplant from California who can never get his car to start and is embarrassed when his brother-in-law has to start it for him.

Interposed between "Winter" and "Spring" is "News," a chapter that operates on two levels. The surface level tells of the Lake Wobegon *Herald-Star*, who reads it, and why. In explaining the appeal of this paper in particular, Keillor explains the appeal of hometown papers everywhere: for many the weekly arrival of the paper is "fresh evidence of a life worth leaving" (250). Much of the chapter covers what needs to be included in the paper, such as detailed accounts of weddings and sports events, and what needs to be omitted, such as anything controversial. Heated arguments at town councils or school board meetings are translated into "discussions" in the news accounts. Everyone in town already knows the details anyway. Far too many people are like Mrs. Magendanz who "steeled herself to do her duty" (65) of minding other people's business.

Keillor injects personal aspects by telling of writing as an imaginative child, of calling home as an adult and being scolded by the switchboard operator who has heard that he flunked out of college, that he is newly divorced. Nevertheless, he is always able to get her to tell him once more about his grandfather, a caring man admired by all. Declaring that he was only bored when he was ill, she launches into a description of that remarkable man who died before the narrator was born.

The second level of the chapter runs along the bottom of every page, ostensibly as an extended footnote but only thinly connected to the surface story. It consists of ninety-five theses written by a native son returned to visit his parents. The writer had planned to nail them to the church door in imitation of Martin Luther, but at the last minute he lacked the courage to do so and shoved them under the door of the newspaper office instead. They are "a dramatic complaint against his upbringing" (251) and, while mainly aimed at his parents, can be seen as an indictment of the community at large. The writer blames his own shortcomings on the way he was reared. Some of the grievances, such as those against bigotry and complacency, are understandable, but others seem meanspirited. Even mean spirit, however, can be seen as a by-product of his training.

The juxtaposition of the ninety-five theses and the amiable account of the town gives the reader a visual picture of a community that is all harmony on the surface while discord and pain beneath. This is the darkest portion of the book. The bitterness of the writer does not lend itself to humor, and the theses are disturbing to read.

"Spring" is doubly welcome after the "News" chapter. Here Keillor is back to his standard characters in established situations. He begins with an account of the Sons of Knute Ice Melt contest, an obvious sign of spring. Clarence Bunsen mentions another sign: "When a bachelor farmer begins to smell himself, you know winter's over" (277). The story that follows explains what happens to overeager farmers who try to get into their fields too soon after the spring thaw. In Lake Wobegon not only does everyone know about mistakes as soon as they happen, but no one ever seems to forget them. Roger Hedlund knows he will be razzed for years about burying his tractor just as Ivan was teased about using too much dynamite in blowing up his dairy barn.

The chapter is filled with activities of spring. Spring cleaning ranges from the annual cabin cleaning conducted by the Sons of Knute to the thorough cleaning of Diane's house by her family. Gardening comes in the form of Mrs. Schwab's yard, Pastor Ingqvist's lawn, and Ella Anderson's flower beds. Yet, as the reader now expects from Keillor, all is not sunshine and singing birds. Ella's story brings the showers that too are a part of spring. The aging Ella, taking care of a senile husband, tries to convince her daughter that things are not as bad as they seem. She wants to remain in her home, yet she is lonely.

Everywhere one can hear music. Piano lessons sound through opened windows. Church choirs rival the singing of birds. Although seventh grade boys sing "America, the Beautiful" with gusto, they are embarrassed when Miss Falconer, their choir director, makes them individually sing lines from an English madrigal. They are self-conscious about their changing voices, their unreliable musicianship, and the suggestive interpretation that can be given to the words. The narrator is so ashamed of his own performance that he will not participate in the evening singing of "Tell Me Why" as he and his sister do the dishes. Instead he goes to his room, puts on a record, and imagines singing a solo to sixty thousand people in Memorial Stadium.

Keillor calls the final chapter "Revival." Much of it centers on the evangelistic services held by Brother Bob and Sister Verna at Lake Wobegon Lutheran Church. Lutheranism has several branches, but it is a reformed denomination, and most reformed denominations display less evangelistic fervor than do fundamentalist groups. The services cause tension in the church, but the evangelists are distant relatives by marriage of Pastor David Ingqvist's wife, and David feels obligated to allow them an annual visit.

His is not the only discomfort in the chapter. It begins with Johnny Tollefson, now home from his first year in college and feeling very out of place. Johnny hopes to be a writer and was elated that the college literary magazine published two of his poems. When he sent a copy of one to his mother, she was not elated; she was furious. Back in Lake Wobegon for the summer, Johnny spends his days writing Whitman-esque poetry as his parents become more and more exasperated with him. On ventures out of his room, he crashes his father's car and visits the Sidetrack Tap. Of the three experiences he thinks necessary in order to write, the only one which seems possible that summer is despair.

There is much of Gary Keillor in Johnny. This is not a first-person narration, but Keillor is very familiar with the anguish of the young writer trying to find his place in a world that does not understand him. He is also familiar with the absurdity of the young writer, however, and does not shirk in revealing Johnny's pretensions and those of some who claim to be writers.

"Revival" means a renewing of life, a restoring to consciousness. After accounts of several people's brushes with death, the final story is of an unnamed man. He too has a near miss when he braves a blizzard to go into town. When he discovers he has forgotten the cigarettes he went for, he does not get angry. What is restored to his consciousness is the realization of how lucky he is to be alive. He thinks: "Some luck lies in not getting what you thought you wanted but getting what you have, which once you have it you may be smart enough to see is what you would have wanted had you known what is really important" (337). For all their foibles, many of the people of Lake Wobegon seem to have reached the same conclusion.

CHARACTER DEVELOPMENT

The ideal short story uses a limited number of characters. The development of those characters may not be as complete as it can be in a longer novel, but the fact that there are only a few individuals to focus on enables the author to reveal character in traditional ways.

Because *Lake Wobegon Days* is not a collection of conventional short stories, however, any discussion of character will likewise not be conventional. What Keillor does in his monologues and later in *Lake Wobegon Days* is create a community. Readers come into that community like outsiders moving into a small town. The new residents first become acquainted with neighbors and business establishments. Gradually they get to know the history of the town and the relationships of the inhabitants. Only after they have lived in the town for a while can they discern change and development in their fellow citizens.

The businesses Keillor mentions most frequently are Ralph's Pretty Good Grocery, Bunsen Motors, the Chatterbox Cafe, and the Sidetrack Tap. They remain constants in both the monologues and the book. Others that are very familiar to radio listeners, such as Bob's Bank, do not appear in the book. Likewise, while Keillor uses some of the names— Ingqvist, Hochstetter, Bunsen—again and again, the names of participants in some of the stories change. For instance, in a monologue he attributes the purchase of an air-conditioner to Mrs. Diener while in *Lake Wobegon Days* Mrs. Hoglund is the person who bought one when there was "nothing wrong with her" (132). The shifts that go back and forth between the spoken and the written word keep the community alive, but they do not make for easy character analysis.

What one can do, however, is group the characters. Even in the first part of the book when Keillor is giving history, he throws in vignettes involving some of the contemporary residents. Many of those residents trace their ancestry back to Magnus Oleson, the first Norwegian settler, but his name seems to have died out. Not so that of Hjalmar Ingqvist. His son Jonson took over his grain business, established the bank, and became important in the state Republican party. Jonson's son Hjalmar was once mayor of Lake Wobegon. He must possess a spark of independence because he drives a Lincoln even though the Ingqvists are Catholic and Catholics drive General Motors cars. His son Chip, who is slightly older than Gary Keillor, is the fourth generation. Chip has the suave self-confidence that comes from established money and prestige in a small town. He wears the right sweaters, uses the right aftershave, and wins honors at state speech contests. Gary wishes to emulate him in everything from his proud condescension to his real speaking ability. It is clear from the topic he speaks on that Garrison Keillor, the writer, is not as impressed with the speeches as Gary Keillor, the student.

Christine, a married daughter of Hjalmar and his wife Virginia, only figures in the book when she visits from California, but David Ingqvist, the Lutheran minister, is a participant in many of the stories. He is a great-nephew of Jonson and thus a second cousin of Chip and Christine. Finally there is Dorene, the Ingqvist cousin from Minneapolis from whom Gary learned more than how to ski.

Another Ingqvist descendant is Birgit Tollefson, who moved back from Honolulu. She is a daughter of Jonson. Her husband's family, the Tollefsons, have been around since the Oskar Tollefson party came back from the Dakotas, but their representatives have been reduced. The only ones to figure prominently in today's Lake Wobegon are Johnny, the boy with the scholarship, and his family.

The first Bavarian immigrant was August Krebsbach, whose progeny seem to be dispersed throughout Lake Wobegon although relationships are not all clear. Florian Krebsbach and his wife Myrtle are the parents of Carl but may be only distantly related to Fred, Hazel, and their daughter Muriel. Hochstetters and Kruegers are other families of German ancestry who are featured in several stories.

Undoubtedly the most familiar name in all of *Lake Wobegon Days* is Bunsen. Clarence and Clint, co-owners of Bunsen Motors, married sisters, Arlene and Irene. The brothers have two uncles—Wally, the baseball player, and Virgil, the estranged relative who dies in Las Vegas. Clarence and Arlene have two daughters, Barbara Ann and Donna, and a son Duane. Barbara Ann was a Keillor fixture before *Lake Wobegon Days*. He began reading letters from her on early radio shows (Lee 13) and eventually turned the letters into *A Prairie Home Companion* monologues that preceded the book.

In the book, however, it is Clarence who is the most fully developed character. He is introduced in the first chapter and mentioned again in the last. In between he comments on the passing scene, on the rich and the poor, on his wife's ancestors and his own. Still Clarence is much more than an observer of the town's events. He cries when he thinks of Barbara Ann's concern for his health, when he receives her unusual gifts. His response is not just emotional, though. He follows her advice and gets more exercise; he eats the *kim chee* she sends. He also wears the red wool serape sent as a gift by his cousin Eddie Bunsen. Clarence is thoughtful and sensitive toward others. He has a sense of justice which serves him when he is asked to handle the funeral arrangements for his Uncle Virgil even though Virgil's own daughter cannot be bothered. Virgil had left Lake Wobegon years earlier after some kind of falling out.

The longstanding alienation leads Clarence to give a homily on letting the sun go down on one's wrath. In so doing, he turns the funeral into an opportunity for reconciliation.

Near the end of the book, Clarence declares, "Somewhere in the world right now, a kid is looking at something and thinking, 'I'm going to remember this for the rest of my life.' And it's the same thing that I looked at forty years ago, whatever it was" (334). Although Clarence is hardly a philosopher, he is not incapable of profound thought. In these words he has summed up the appeal of *Lake Wobegon Days* to many readers.

THEMATIC ISSUES

Although Garrison Keillor has been accused of describing Lake Wobegon and its residents in nostalgic terms (Fiske), what he really presents in *Lake Wobegon Days* is a complete community with both charm and ugliness, strength and limitation. On the same cold night beautifully described as having "the volume of the world . . . turned up" (237), he pictures the Sidetrack Tap with the *R* missing from its neon sign. The flashing red "BEE . . . BEE . . . BEE" gives a discordant contrast with the white of the snowy night.

The characters range from children to the elderly, and while Keillor finds humor in their eccentricities, he also shows their pain. The boy who hates being chosen last for recess baseball games is not too different from the immigrants who dream of Norway "where they were young and full of hope" (65). Now they are old and hampered by English, a language learned in midlife and never fully mastered. As they look back to their youth, so the boy looks toward adulthood. Neither is satisfied with the present.

Keillor's presentation of traditional virtues such as pride and loyalty shows equal inclusiveness. The chapter "Forebears" explores both positive and negative aspects of pride in relation to a prospective visit by the king of Norway. The ethnic pride responsible for town cleanup is admirable, but the umbrage taken by the Rognes family when they were not included in plans for a small coffee demonstrates a pride even their son finds excessive. In donating a church furnace in their memory, he admits, "I always thought—if pride were kindling, our family could heat the church for twenty years" (89). In "Sumus Quod Sumus" Keillor treats loyalty in much the same way. While showing the loyalty most Lake

Wobegonians have to local merchants, he also shows at what cost that loyalty comes. Those who purchase locally sacrifice style and thrift as well as variety.

Other traditional virtues are presented as negatives because they are excessive. Judy Ingqvist's refusal to sing out in choir even though she has a lovely voice is humility in the extreme. Here Keillor seems to be saying that those who do not use their talent must take responsibility for the mediocrity that results. Likewise when people in Lake Wobegon interpret the word *smart* as meaning smart aleck, mediocre intellectual pursuits seem also to be the order of the day. Both of these examples are given in "Sumus Quod Sumus" and seem appropriate to the "warts and all" presentation of Lake Wobegon and its slogan, "We are what we are."

ALTERNATE READING: MAGICAL REALISM

Magical realism is a term coined in 1925 by German critic Franz Roh. Roh used it to describe the work of certain artists who returned to a kind of realistic painting after the abstraction of Expressionism (15–31). Gradually the term began to be applied to literature as well. Angel Flores credits Jorge Luis Borge with introducing magical realism to Latin America in 1935. Shortly after Borge finished Spanish translations of Franz Kafka's short stories, he began to incorporate the magically real into his own writing. Since then magical realism in Latin American literature has grown in what Flores calls "an exciting crescendo" (113). Today the term *magical realism* is used in discussing the work of such diverse writers as Salman Rushdie and Toni Morrison, Umberto Eco and Ben Okri.

In magical realism a work of literature is conventional on the surface while unconventional beneath. The unconventional elements can be those of myth, folklore, the supernatural, or fantasy. Luis Leal explains, "The magical realist does not try to copy the surrounding reality (as the realists did) or to wound it (as the Surrealists did) but to seize the mystery that breathes behind things" (123). The mysterious elements contrast with the realistic framework of the literature, causing an unreal blending. In some novels, those of Gabriel García Márquez for instance, that contrast comes because of the merging of an essentially European culture with a more superstitious one, which accepts the supernatural. "The presence of the supernatural is often attributed to the primitive or 'magical' Indian mentality, which coexists with European rationality" (Chanady 19).

At least one critic has used the label *magical realism* in connection with *Lake Wobegon Days* (Reed). The collision in this book is not between primitive and rational cultures but between the ordinary and the extraordinary. Ordinary characters and events are the basis of realism. Identification with ordinary emotions and situations produces recognition for the reader, but the reader has no difficulty accepting the extraordinary. Wendy B. Faris maintains that "magical realism combines realism and the fantastic in such a way that magical elements grow organically out of the reality portrayed" (163). That seems to be the case in *Lake Wobegon Days*.

Confrontations between the real and the unreal begin with the account of the first settlement of Lake Wobegon. The concept of missionaries from Massachusetts going to the Great Lakes area to convert Indians to Christianity is a very real picture of what actually happened on the frontier. The means used—interpretive dance—is not. Equally unreal is the marriage between Prudence, one of the missionaries, and Basile, the French trapper who eats half-raw bear meat and sleeps with his dogs. His singing bawdy songs and going to the toilet in public are counterposed with Prudence's composition of sonnets using the letters of his name.

"Sumus Quod Sumus" describes the contemporary town with its statue of the Unknown Norwegian. The subject may be unusual, but a statue is to be expected in the center of a small town. What is not to be expected is its distinguishing characteristic—the quackgrass that keeps growing out of its ear.

"Fall" tells the tragedy of Pete Peterson, for whom a memorial duck blind is named. Pete, terrified of getting cancer, kept a list of danger signs on the mirror in his bathroom and daily looked for some telltale change in himself. When he felt a lump on his head, he panicked and, on a frantic drive to see a doctor, crashed into a gravel truck. His story is offset by a description of the duck blind. It uses fourteen-foot giant duck decoys built on the theory that ducks cannot see decoys that are life-sized.

In "Winter" the realistic picture of a boy who mopes around trying to get his family's attention and sympathy is juxtaposed against the fantasy of a boy killed by an icicle. In his book bag are his assignments, all correctly done. Such contrasts continue throughout the book as Keillor merges the real and the unreal in a magical way.

5

Leaving Home
(1987)

Leaving Home, Garrison Keillor's third book, consists of an introduction, thirty-five stories, and a short final chapter in which Keillor bids good-bye to his fictional hometown of Lake Wobegon, Minnesota. Although *Lake Wobegon Days*, his previous book, reworks material used on radio broadcasts of *A Prairie Home Companion*, *Leaving Home* differs in that it is made up of transcriptions of specific monologues. Three of them—"A Trip to Grand Rapids," "The Killer," and "Chicken"—appeared in the *Atlantic*, but they were all meant to be spoken. Keillor says, "They were written for my voice, which is flat and slow. There are long pauses in them and sentences that trail off into the raspberry bushes" (xvi).

At the time *Leaving Home* was published, Keillor had just ended thirteen years of *A Prairie Home Companion* in order to live in Denmark with his new wife, a native of that country. After a short stay he returned to the United States, and eventually he returned to broadcasting. However, in 1987 he had every reason to believe that his career in the United States was at an end.

In "Introduction: A Letter from Copenhagen," Keillor says nothing is better than fresh sweet corn, and he would perhaps still be in Minnesota if he had eaten more of it. But he "lost touch with people who raised corn" (xv). He was bothered by changes in Minnesota, such as the growth of soulless megamalls where once small farms and produce stands had flourished. St. Paul, like Lake Wobegon, had seemed to him "a gentler place, shaded from predators" (xv) until the local newspaper printed details of his personal life. Then he came to the conclusion that his life would probably be better lived somewhere else. He wrote "A Letter from Copenhagen" on July 3, 1987, less than a month after he moved to Denmark.

The monologues in *Leaving Home* are loosely arranged to cover twelve consecutive months, beginning around the time of spring planting and ending in April of the following year. The stories each stand alone, but taken together, they give a vivid picture of life in Lake Wobegon. With one exception, "The Royal Family," each of them begins with the familiar line: "It has been a quiet week in Lake Wobegon" although sometimes the news from Lake Wobegon is anything but quiet. In one story Carl Krebsbach discovers that his father's septic tank is a 1937 Chevy with its roof squashed in. He ends up hauling it down main street during the homecoming parade. In another tale, when town deputies Gary and Leroy stop a doctor for speeding, he gives them a drug that reverses the effects of aging.

Keillor's good-natured humor and keen understanding of people are threaded throughout the book, poignantly reflecting the failures and successes of the characters. He knows that many aspects of human nature are the same, no matter the location of the humans. It is this quality in Keillor's storytelling that appeals to his audience. As Keillor says, "Life is complicated and not for the timid. It's an experience that when it's done, it will take us a while to get over it" (xv).

PLOT DEVELOPMENT

Because the stories in *Leaving Home* began as oral presentations, their plot development is often erratic, reflecting the element of conversation in which they are told. In some stories there is no obvious plot, no conflict and resolution, but simply a recounting of something that has happened to one of the characters. In other stories Keillor takes detours, goes down one road and then another much as people do in actual conversation. Often he brings all the routes together, but sometimes he leaves the ending open, and the reader may wonder what the destination is. Occasionally the journey itself seems to be the destination. When this is the case, the reader simply enjoys the ride.

Man versus nature is one of the classic conflicts on which plot is based. One element of nature is weather. Although the weather is not really an antagonist in "A Trip to Grand Rapids," the first story in *Leaving Home*, it lies at the root of all the problems. Wind is responsible for the errant sign that almost bisects Mr. Lundberg, for the falling ceiling that brings down on his head recriminations from his wife along with bits of plaster. Because of rain Roger Hedlund finds himself outside hunting for a kitten in the middle of the night and wading through fields too wet to bear the weight of his tractor. In this particular wet spring, rain prevents Roger from working and sets up the secondary conflicts with his daughters.

"A Ten-Dollar Bill" centers around family conflict between Senator K. Thorvaldson and the cousin's family with whom he shares a two-bedroom Florida condominium and between Senator's great nephew Jim and Jim's father. For Senator the last straw comes when his cousin's wife moves him to the hide-a-bed to make room for her visiting aunt. Finding sleep difficult with a "hide-a-crossbar" (12) in his back and a hostile dog across the room, Senator decides to return to Lake Wobegon earlier than planned. He sends that news to Jim along with an early birthday money order designed to compensate for the parsimony of Jim's father.

Easter is a time of rebirth and renewal. The monologue entitled "Easter" is less a story than a meditation on the idea of renewal through children. Keillor begins it with remembrances of his own childhood when he had difficulty sitting still in church and then discusses various approaches to bringing up children. Realizing that parents would be terrified if they were aware of everything their children did, he surmises that "selective ignorance" is "a cornerstone of child rearing" (19). He ends the monologue with another incident from his own childhood, about a fishing trip with his Uncle Al, and concludes, "Nothing you do for children is ever wasted" (20).

In "Corinne" Senator K. Thorvaldson is picked up at the airport and taken to Lake Wobegon by Corinne Inqvist, daughter of the local bank president. The story portion dealing with Senator K. details his return from Florida anticipated in "A Ten-Dollar Bill" and mentions a woman from Maine to whom he has proposed. While those are continuations of stories told elsewhere, Corinne's story is new. Corinne is a talented teacher whose values differ from those of her father. The conflict occurs when she asks him for a loan to buy a house.

"A Glass of Wendy" is named for the most popular order at the Sidetrack Tap. Another monologue that is more meditation than story, it gives the background of Saint Wendell's beer and the Dimmers family that produced it. More important ruminations have to do with fitting tributes for life achievements. Clarence Bunsen has just received one more ugly plaque to commemorate the many years Bunsen Motors has been in business. Father Emil, the priest of Our Lady of Perpetual Responsibility, plans to retire after forty years. Clarence suggests to Wally, the bartender, that the community could send Father Emil to Jamaica, a place the priest is eager to visit. Wally's reaction makes it clear that Father Emil is not likely to get his trip.

A smooth con artist takes on the town in "The Speeding Ticket." Stopped by Gary and Leroy, Lake Wobegon's policemen, for streaking through town at sixty-five miles per hour, Dr. Walter W. Ingersoll, supposedly from a biomedical laboratory in Ontario, is most apologetic, particularly because he might have killed a child. He explains that had he not been talking on his car phone to the University of Chicago where he was rushing the experimental drug *belostalone*, he would surely have seen the town and its speed limit signs. His insinuation that his listeners cannot understand a medical explanation of the drug makes them insist that he give one. His insistence that he compensate them for potential loss by giving them free samples makes them pay him $20 per vial. Only after he leaves do they realize that the whole thing was a scam. Nevertheless, they all feel better and are mostly concerned not that they wasted $20 on a fake rejuvenation drug but that they do not know where to find him to get more.

"Seeds" is not a story; it is a homily to spring. Seeds take on symbolic meaning to those who live in Minnesota, where winter always lasts too long. Seeds bring the earth out of the torpor of winter and remind them that the earth will bloom again.

The plot in "Chicken" hinges on subtle conflicts between country ways and city ways and between vegetarian and carnivorous eating habits. To Dad and Aunt Flo, both reared on a farm, killing chickens to eat is natural. Flo once tried cooking processed fryers and was appalled by the quality of meat from force-fed chickens kept cooped up in the dark. She returned to killing her own chickens. On butchering day Uncle Al, a city boy, makes himself absent. Mother shares Al's urban background but gamely participates by dipping the butchered chickens into boiling water and plucking them. Keillor, in the persona he assumes for the monologues, has only one job. He catches the chickens and hands them to his father, who chops off their heads. Before they finish, Keillor faces a dilemma. If he plans to continue eating meat, he thinks he should be able to kill a chicken. For Aunt Flo, home butchery stands for quality; for him it stands for honesty. If he cannot face life and death, he had "better stick to celery" (46).

When Becky Diener is assigned to write a 750-word essay on her backyard as if she were seeing it for the first time, she is stumped. In "How the Crab Apple Grew," she gazes at the yard and a tree that has just burst into bloom. Becky remembers only that her father brought home the tree when she was six. Her attempts at writing the composition do no justice to the assignment or the backyard, but Keillor captures exactly the way too many high school students write.

Leaving Becky to discard one repetitive draft after another, Keillor moves back in time to tell the story of the flowering crab and the courtship of Becky's parents. Harold and Marlys Diener may not seem to be a romantic couple today, but their story involves Harold's rivalry with a geography teacher, a rivalry that he won by bringing Marlys morel mushrooms and a bouquet of flowering crab. After ten years of marriage, when the romance had definitely faded, Harold revitalized the relationship by bringing a crab branch from the forest and grafting it onto a root in the backyard. The result was a magnificent tree. Keillor concludes, "A backyard is a novel about us, and when we sit there on a summer day, we hear the dialogue and see the characters" (54).

"Truckstop" continues the subject of marital relationships and their inevitable tensions. On a trip to Minneapolis to take his wife Myrtle to the doctor, Florian Krebsbach is terrified of the huge trucks that speed by them on the interstate. Myrtle, who is convinced she has cancer no local doctor can detect, rails at her mate of forty-eight years when he suggests returning home. Florian stops to get coffee and inadvertently leaves Myrtle at the truck stop. His ensuing attempts to find his way back to the truck stop and then home are simultaneously sad and amusing. The resolution solves their problem with a nice twist.

When Carla Krebsbach thinks it would be nice if the Class of '86 had just eighty-six graduates instead of eighty-seven, she realizes that her thought is almost like wishing someone were dead. The yearbook picture she is looking at when she has that thought is of Dale Uecker. He becomes the subject of "Dale," one of Keillor's rambling monologues. When Carla tells him after commencement, "I'm awfully glad you're alive" (65), Dale is completely unaware of her reason. What he feels is an affirmation of what he wrote earlier in his own yearbook: "I AM ALIVE ... THE IMPORTANT THING IS LIFE ITSELF" (65). He wrote it as a kind of defense when he thought he would not graduate with his class, but he can still answer Carla, "It's enough to be alive, . . . a person doesn't need anything else" (65).

The rest of the monologue follows Dale through his good-byes as he leaves for the navy. Joining was a decision he made on his own. It has upset his family and scared him, but at the same time he is exhilarated by the act of leaving and facing the unknown future. That, Keillor seems to be saying, is what being alive is all about.

Once again it is Lake Wobegon against the weather in "High Rise." This time hot weather has brought out mosquitos. Ella Anderson coats herself with repellant before she works outside, and Father Emil plants onions to prevent mosquito bites, but Myrtle Krebsbach has a plan to outsmart the mosquitos. She is trying to convince her husband Florian to move to a senior citizen high-rise. She has read that mosquitoes do not rise above the third floor. Florian, however, has a fear of heights and no interest in moving from the farm where he was born. His attempts to thwart her wishes result in interpersonal conflict as well. For two years, ever since a fight with her sister-in-law, Myrtle has talked about moving, and for two years Florian has worked to more firmly entrench himself at the farm. He started raising ducks. He began buying old furniture and farm equipment at auctions.

There is no resolution to the conflict of the Krebsbachs, now in their seventies. The monologue ends instead with a joke, one of many that Florian recounts to his ducks. It tells of two senior citizens who finally file for divorce after outliving their children, explaining that even though they have detested each other for fifty years, they did not consider the step sooner because their divorce would have killed their offspring!

For a few seconds Clarence Bunsen thinks he is having a heart attack. The experience and its aftermath are told in "Collection." His brush with mortality leads Clarence to question everything from underwear and breakfast choices to church attendance. He goes to church as usual, but an error when he writes a check for the offering makes Clarence realize that he plans to be around for a long time to come.

Clarence probably concludes that "Life Is Good," the title of the next monologue, although that account is not about the Bunsens but the Tolleruds. In one of the funniest stories in the collection, Keillor tells about Daryl's conflict with his father, a man who hates plans. Even when he has made them himself, he feels trapped by them and tries to temporize right up until the time for action. It is a character trait that drives Daryl crazy.

The situation comes to a head when a projected visit to Seattle with all plans made is threatened by the old man's equivocation. Daryl's mother has told him about a letter should something happen to them in Seattle. Convinced by his father's treatment that the letter will tell him he is adopted, the forty-two-year-old Daryl takes advantage of his parents' absence to search for the letter. He does not find it, but in the middle of the slapstick action, he comes to the realization that he has been annoyed by trivialities, that life is indeed very good.

In "Lyle's Roof" the conflict lies within Lyle. He feels himself a failure despite success as a high school science teacher. His feeling of inadequacy comes from being surrounded by handy individuals like his brother-in-law Carl Krebsbach. Carl's good-natured offers of help with the plumbing or household repairs produce resentment, not gratitude. Lyle is filled with guilt because he thinks he should be able to fix such things himself. Keillor digresses to tell other stories about guilt and to give the history of Lyle's house, which explains why it needs so many repairs. Then he returns to Lyle's predicament. In substituting for an ill teacher in a speech class, he hears his daughter talk about the love of her family. That reminder of the warmth of home gives him the courage to ask Carl to help fix his house.

Wally of the Sidetrack Tap has taken to the water in "Pontoon Boat." He is so pleased with his new purchase that he asks everyone he sees to take a ride. When he extends the invitation to Clint Bunsen, Lake Wobegon's mayor, Clint remembers that a group of Lutheran ministers is arriving on Friday. They are touring the area to assess the "pastoral needs" in rural areas, but Clint thinks inviting them for a cookout on the boat will be preferable to talking to clergymen about municipal problems. Thus twenty-four ministers are taken from their bus to Wally's twenty-six-foot boat. When Wally lights the grill and the preachers move away from the heat, the boat predictably capsizes. The story has so resolution. In fact, it is less a story than a recounting of a funny incident with some devastating descriptions of the clergy, who have "more eye contact than you were really looking for, . . . more affirmation than you needed" (106).

"State Fair," the only story that takes place outside Lake Wobegon, is a personal reminiscence. Keillor recalls the sights, sounds, and odors of the State Fair. He and his family attended it every year when he was growing up, and he vividly remembers how it was. He always had to wear "fundamentalist clothes" because he had to sing in the gospel tent. As Christians, his family carefully avoided the temptations of the Midway, but for Keillor the mere proximity of sin was exciting. He tells of the time his aunt entered a cake-baking contest and what it was like to ride the Ferris wheel at the end of summer. The view he gets as the wheel turns and he looks down from above is unforgettable. He gives an adult's interpretation of a child's epiphany and concludes, as in a previous story, that life is indeed good.

In "David and Agnes, a Romance," Keillor begins with the inclusion in the local paper of a ten-year-old thank you. The assumption that it is current leads to some funny conclusions, but the story leads Keillor into one about Val and Florence Tollefson. In 1946 Val's father David ran off with another man's wife. Eighteen-year-old Val was devastated. He destroyed everything his father had ever given him. Now, forty years later, David has died and Val has inherited a trunk with his father's possessions. When the trunk arrives, Val is curious about its contents. He finds certificates for faithful service to a church in his new community and a Bible with the names of David and Agnes. For all these years Val has never known the name of the "other woman." Val finds himself very curious about two people who could challenge all of Lake Wobegon's norms. What kind of man could abandon a wife and five children? What kind of woman would leave behind her own two offspring? What attraction compelled two responsible people to take such drastic steps? Val finds all their love letters, many folded as though they were once hidden. He reads all of them plus a poem and then destroys them though not before Florence rescues the poem.

"The Killer" is a spoof of horror movies with a personal digression in the middle about Keillor's experiences as president of the Young People's Bible Study. Lake Wobegon in October provides the wet, bone-chilling weather of stereotypical horror settings, making it the perfect time to preview *The Hand Under the Bed*, a new movie in which one of Lake Wobegon's own, Barb Diener, has a bit part. In describing her career since leaving home, Keillor makes fun of California lifestyles in the sixties and seventies as well as small-town reaction to minor fame.

As a contrast to the rain of "The Killer," the next monologue "Eloise" is set amid magnificent fall colors—"reds and yellows, oranges, some so brilliant that Crayola never put them in crayons for fear the children would color outside the lines"(133). The protagonist is the daughter of Myrtle and Florian Krebsbach. After a divorce, Eloise could not afford to remain in Minneapolis, but she is a misfit in Lake Wobegon. Her family is embarrassed that she receives welfare to support her three children. Eloise feels herself pitted against Lake Wobegon convention. In an attempt to become independent, she takes out an ad offering dancing lessons. An unlikely taker is Ella Anderson, the elderly woman who is trying to maintain her own independence by caring for her senile husband in their own home. Ella thinks dancing may help her hip. Keillor concludes with a picture through a window of the two women waltzing, framed by the bright autumn colors.

"The Royal Family" tells of another daughter of Lake Wobegon, Grace Tollefson, who ran off with Alex Campbell, a ne'er-do-well with an appealing manner and no substance. When he left her after twelve years of marriage and three children, she too returned to Lake Wobegon. There she lives in a mobile home behind her brother's house, struggling to survive on the charity of relatives and the Lutheran church.

One day, a letter comes from a man named D. R. MacKay. In it, he tells Grace that her children are the direct descendants of the throne of Scotland, and he is working to restore their legacy. Grace tells the children but cautions them to say nothing of it to anyone. However, the knowledge gives them pride and makes them feel less dependent. When Grace's brother Lawrence suggests that she is not being properly grateful and consequently should start supporting herself, Grace takes the children and moves back to St. Paul. Life is often bleak for them, but the occasional letters from Mr. MacKay provide encouragement. They give Grace and the children the inspiration to continue. The story has a not unexpected twist at the end.

Every fall homecoming football games and parades are popularly attended events all across America. In "Homecoming" Carl Krebsbach has every intention of attending the parade to see his daughter Carla reign as queen—that is until an emergency call from his father Florian. Although this is a very funny story, the underlying conflict is between parental duty and filial duty. It is a choice faced more and more frequently today as the population ages. Carl chooses logically; he responds to the greatest need, his father's. That need is to replace a septic tank. When he finds out that what has been used all these years is an old car, he is appalled, but doggedly removes it and carts it away only to end up in the parade he thought he would miss.

Not that Lake Wobegon's parades are ever exactly like everyone else's. Because a brother of the organizing teacher is a colonel in the National Guard, the queen traditionally rides in a Sherman tank. In an aside, Keillor admits that such an association may have affected his attitude toward beautiful women. Carl's inadvertent addition of the car does spice up the parade, however. Despite Carla's embarrassment, it becomes the most memorable of Lake Wobegon's homecomings.

Although "Brethren" begins with some discussion of Halloween, it is really about peacemaking. The Sanctified Brethren are a fractious group, always splitting into factions over minor points of faith. Keillor's Uncle

Al tries to settle one dispute by inviting two contenders to dinner. They bring their rivalry to the dinner table where each tries to outpray the other. Fortunately, the smell of Aunt Flo's fried chicken conquers both.

In "Thanksgiving" Pastor Ingqvist is surprised that the church is almost full for the holiday service. Everyone seems to have come to church this year, everyone but Clarence Bunsen, who is feeling depressed about several things. His back hurts and his hair is falling out, but more important, he has a premonition that the real reason his daughter Barbara Ann is coming for the holidays is to announce that she and her husband Bill are getting a divorce. In addition, there is a nagging remembrance that when his wife Arlene wanted to eat Thanksgiving dinner out, he offered to cook the meal. The conflict is between Clarence and himself— his fallibility, his imagination, his reluctance to change. His difficulties are compounded by a malfunctioning fireplace. At the end most of the conflicts are not resolved; they just disappear when Clarence discovers that the announcement Barbara Ann has come to make is not of a divorce but of a baby on the way.

For thirteen years Darlene has been a waitress at the Chatterbox Cafe. She has been like a comfortable spouse to her regular customers, who are shattered at the prospect of her leaving. Yet in "Darlene Makes a Move," she does just that. All her life her mother has been after her, asking why she does not do something with herself. In the past the question always precipitated a brief internal struggle, brief because she was always able to think of someone who tried whatever she was considering. The outcome did not appeal to her. Only when her mother asks, "Oh, honey, why didn't you ever do something with yourself?" (170) is she startled out of her complacency enough to move on.

The two monologues, "Christmas Dinner" and "Exiles," have to do with holiday gatherings. Keillor visits two homes in "Christmas Dinner." Both have internal conflicts. At Clarence and Arlene Bunsen's, their daughter Donna has come with her family from California. Her husband Rick criticizes women, Norwegians, and Democrats. Although Arlene finds him obnoxious, she hesitates to tell him so because of her grandchildren. Instead she neutralizes him by stuffing him with food at every opportunity. In the second family, the Tolleruds, there is another glimpse of the tension between Daryl and his father, already seen in "Life is Good." Of the three brothers gathered with their families at the large parental home, Daryl is the only one who stayed in Lake Wobegon. Clearly his father has taken advantage of Daryl. In 1968 he went into partnership with the old man on the understanding that he would eventually take over both the farm and the large house while his parents would move to Daryl's small residence, the original Tollerud homestead. Nevertheless, after all these years, his father still gives the orders, and Daryl's six children are crammed into the little house. The humorous episode here involves mincemeat pie. It has a nice resolution, but at the end of the monologue, the conflict remains.

The "Exiles" describes some of the natives who return to Lake Wobegon for the holidays. They include Larry the Sad Boy, Eddie the Jealous Boy, and Foxy the Proud Boy. The central exile, however, is Corinne Ingqvist. A teacher in Minneapolis, she brings along 132 student essays to grade. In another story of contending obligations, she realizes that the opportunities to spend time with her aging parents may be numbered, and she puts her professional duties aside, at least for this brief visit.

The Christmas monologues are about return, but "New Year's" centers on escape. Those attempting to get away are the Reverend David Ingqvist and his wife Judy. Standing in their way are the members of his congregation at Lake Wobegon Lutheran Church, who can see no reason why their minister should go to the Annual Minister's Retreat if it is held on Captiva Island. Judy could give them several reasons, but doing so would reveal more than the church wants to know about its minister. Other things from a faltering furnace and flu to invasion by fleas and mice intensify their need to leave. They finally manage the trip, local disapproval notwithstanding.

"Where Did It Go Wrong?" starts with a discussion of an epidemic of Swedish flu. Keillor explains that it is similar to Asian flu except that those suffering from it assume it is their fault. He details the chaos in the Diener home when both parents are extremely ill and moves on to the Ash Wednesday service at Our Lady of Perpetual Responsibility. Father Emil leaves his sickbed to conduct the service. Keillor comments that observing Ash Wednesday when so many people have flu is "to be in a state of redundant contrition" (198). That leads into a discussion of original sin, where it all went wrong in the first place. Loosely linked is the final tale of Darlene, who has now made her move to Minneapolis. One of her objectives was to find her long-gone husband Arlen and file for divorce. She muses about their marriage and wonders where it went wrong.

One of the disadvantages of living in a town as small as Lake Wobegon is that everyone knows everyone else's business. For that reason, Bud is mortified when a sudden drop in temperature catches him with no antifreeze in his truck. Because his job as maintenance man for the community would make his neglect doubly embarrassing, Bud goes to another town to buy a radiator to replace the one that is now cracked.

His distress is only one produced by the sudden cold snap. "Post Office" details the frustration of the newspaper editor, the chagrin of the Ingqvists, and the discomfort of all who have their mail examined by others. When it is too cold for the postmaster to sort the mail, he puts it out so that everyone can rummage through and find his or her own. What most people find is the interesting-looking mail of their neighbors. They do not take it, but it fuels their imaginations, first in fantasizing about their acquaintances and then in becoming suspicious of the postmaster and all who may have looked at their own mail. Keillor concludes with observations about the need for privacy.

Minnesotans continue to battle the elements in the next monologue although "Out in the Cold" also has a figurative meaning. Mr. Odegaard, a bachelor farmer, attempts to walk home from the Sidetrack Tap when his pickup refuses to start. He is unsuccessful in his attempts to thumb a ride. The various people who pass him by—the postmaster, student evangelists from Georgia, and the Bishop of Brainerd—are all out in the cold in their own way.

"Hawaii," a monologue broadcast from that state, is an examination of envy and guilt. In it Keillor claims to be the first person from Lake Wobegon to actually make the trip to Hawaii though several have almost gone. He chronicles their tales and explains why people never seem to go: "This was Minnesota, they were Lutherans, and you didn't just fly over to Hawaii for your own pleasure because you wanted to. It wasn't right" (217). Instead people from Lake Wobegon would have to have a reason to go, to make it seem that they could not get out of going. Keillor concludes, "My people aren't paradise people" (217). He believes they will be uncomfortable in heaven as well.

"Hansel" is a tribute to the art of storytelling. Kenny is supposed to be babysitting his five youngsters while his wife is at choir practice. The story he tells them, about Hansel and Gretel, gets mixed up in the monologue with the story of Kenny's own father and stepmother. Keillor stresses that no matter how familiar a story, no one knows for sure what will happen. Relief comes when, in both Kenny's life and the story he tells, things turn out satisfactorily.

Intramarital strife is the focus of "Du, Du Liegst Mir in Herzen." Somehow Gene and Lois Pfleiderscheidt have endured fifty years of marriage despite complaining about each other to anyone who would listen. Their golden wedding celebration is no different from other days. They spend the evening denigrating each other until their daughters finally get them to dance. Then it is apparent what has held them together for so long.

The Canterbury Tales begins with a description of spring. "Aprille" begins with a recitation of that description. To residents of Lake Wobegon, hearing high school students struggle with those lines in Chaucer's Middle English is one sign of spring. Another sign is Confirmation Sunday at Lake Wobegon Lutheran. Keillor puts himself into this monologue as godfather of a confirmand, Lois Tollerud. He tells of his favorite aunt, for whom he named Lois, and describes bus trips with her when they pretended they were strangers. He concludes that although all people become strangers, some things, like the characteristics of April, remain constant.

"Goodbye to the Lake" is Keillor's farewell monologue on what he thought would be his last broadcast of *A Prairie Home Companion*. It is raining in Lake Wobegon. Keillor gives glimpses of various familiar characters and concludes with several of them gathered at the Chatterbox Cafe. He says he will remember them that way as he leaves for Copenhagen. He expects the reader to remember them that way too.

CHARACTER DEVELOPMENT

Characters in the monologues often prove resistant to any methodical analysis because they appear here and there in different stories without logical sequence. There are more than 150 characters in *Leaving Home*. Many of them can be grouped into families, but sometimes Keillor uses only a first name, making the character's relationship to other characters unclear. The establishment of exact kinship is often not important to Keillor; it is the story that interests him most.

These monologues were all originally directed at listeners rather than readers. Keillor tries to make his radio audience comfortable by using familiar names, but because immediate credibility is more crucial than long-term continuity, he does develop some inconsistencies. For instance, in "Exiles," Corinne Ingqvist tells her mother she will never have children. Virginia accepts that statement philosophically and responds, "I'll never be a grandma" (186). Yet in "Easter" the Ingqvists are hosting two grandchildren, Doug and Danielle, offspring of their daughter Barbara. In "Hawaii" the Ingqvists attempt to take Stanley, another grandson, on vacation with them. Which of their own children has produced Stanley is not explained, nor do Chip and Christine, Hjalmar and Virginia's children in *Lake Wobegon Days*, ever appear in this book.

Some characters from the earlier book take on more prominent roles in *Leaving Home*, however. David and Judy Ingqvist, the Lutheran minister and his wife, are such characters. They are very human here, not the paragons of virtue their parishioners want them to be. As is the case with most people in their line of work, David and Judy feel the pressure of being constantly under the eye of the congregation. Church members do not confine their advice to trying to get David to liven up the church services, but make it clear that they know what is best for everything from home maintenance to his personal life. As a result, he and Judy take out their frustrations on each other. When in "Pontoon Boat" he forgets to tell her that a group of Lutheran ministers is coming for a picnic, she declines to come to his rescue. He can serve wieners and perhaps he can find someone to make some potato salad. In "Exiles" when Hjalmar, Virginia, and Corinne arrive unexpectedly, David and Judy are in the midst of an argument.

David is not unperceptive, however. He knows very well that both he and Judy need to get away, to spend time by themselves and with other pastors and their wives, people who understand their situation. "New Year's" and "Post Office" discuss their attempts to attend the Annual Ministers' Retreat for the first time in three years. In the latter monologue, Judy is devastated when members of the building committee, down in the parsonage basement to analyze the failing furnace, see her pink underwear drying on the line. Even though the underwear was dyed when something red got into the wash load, she knows they will hesitate to authorize trip money for a minister's wife who buys frivolous underwear, particularly when the church will soon need to pay for furnace repairs. In "New Year's" Judy is finding it more and more difficult to smile up at her husband in the pulpit when he says something she thinks is dumb. By the time she weathers fleas, mice, and their children's flu, Judy is almost defeated. Her dejection moves David to decision. He quickly arranges for Judy's mother to babysit and gets them out of a situation that has almost overwhelmed them both. David is a humane individual, as is evidenced by his continually catching a mouse in a live trap only to have it return, but he is usually more a man of thought than a man of action. Yet in this instance he proves that not only does he care about his wife, but he acts on that concern. Someone who is not discouraged by the sometimes sparse attendance at his church services is not easily daunted by a depressed wife. He just keeps doing his job, buoyed by the faith that led him to this profession in the first place.

Father Emil, priest of Our Lady of Perpetual Responsibility, is David Ingqvist's Catholic counterpart. Father Emil is close to retirement after having served the parish for forty-four years. He has had little vacation, no pension, and no provisions made for his old age. He naively trusts in his bishop to see to his care when the time comes. Father Emil has quietly tended to the needs of his parish for almost half a century, making so few demands that the bishop is not even aware of the small church's existence until Father Emil's impending retirement. After he gets cancer, Father Emil gets up out of his sickbed to conduct Christmas Eve mass. By Ash Wednesday, he has a replacement, but when the replacement gets the flu, Father Emil again does the service. His sense of duty always wins out over his own best interest.

Florian and Myrtle Krebsbach are other characters more completely developed here than in *Lake Wobegon Days*. Florian owns a garage, Krebsbach's Chevrolet, but appears not to have much of a head for business. This year's inventory never agrees with last year's, and his desk is a disaster area. However, having survived this long, he will not worry about it now. Florian epitomizes the word "conservative." He has only forty-seven thousand miles on his 1966 Chevrolet, which he drives at forty miles an hour even on the interstate. It is his plodding character that provides the humor in "Truckstop." His wife Myrtle mistakes his oversight for passionate anger and is flattered. Nevertheless, he does not like change and is happy with things the way they are, both at work and at home.

Not so Myrtle, who agitates for change in "High Rise." Myrtle is not the stereotypical Midwestern housewife of seventy-odd years. While Florian tries to avoid confrontation, she thrives on it. While he is mild in both manner and speech, she has a gland in her throat that "secretes profanity" (75). Once she slapped her sister-in-law Beatrice in an altercation over a family heirloom. When Myrtle was forced by her sisters to apologize, she whispered curses in Beatrice's ear as they embraced.

The Krebsbachs' son Carl is a reliable and steady man who figures in five of the monologues. Carl's occupation is never given, but he is obviously a capable individual with the ability to do whatever needs to be done. As a result, he is called upon by his parents, his brother-in-law, and his neighbors whenever they need help with repairs or odd jobs. Usually Carl is a willing helper, but occasionally there are so many demands on his time that he feels envy for those who are incompetent.

Clarence Bunsen remains one of Keillor's favorite characters, and he often has a walk-on role in stories that are not about him. As in *Lake Wobegon Days*, he is in the first chapter and the last and many in between. Clarence is presented as a middle-aged man who is beginning to worry. The focus of his concern varies from his business or his health to his family, specifically his daughter Barbara Ann.

With his brother Clint, the mayor of Lake Wobegon, Clarence owns Bunsen Motors, the local Ford dealership. When business is slow and he finds he will be forced to borrow $7,000 to meet one month's expenses, he is justifiably concerned. He also has experienced some physical problems that he thinks must be related to his heart. Even though he says nothing to his wife Arlene, he begins walking in the early mornings, hoping that exercise will help.

Although Clarence never seems to fret about his daughter Donna, he has always had a soft spot for Barbara Ann. His concern about her is a constant, but the other concerns are new and can probably be attributed to the fact that he is getting older. The effects of aging—back problems and thinning hair—discourage him so much that even coffee, the Norwegian cure-all, gives no help.

Keillor writes about Minnesotans, a great number of whom are of Scandinavian or German descent, and ascribes to them certain characteristics: Lutherans find it difficult to enjoy themselves; old Norwegian bachelors can be testy; farmers constantly worry about weather and are never satisfied with it or their crops; Catholics carry around a heavy burden of guilt and duty. These are generalizations, but they carry enough truth to provide a basis for some of Keillor's funniest material.

THEMATIC ISSUES

Not every monologue carries the same theme, but most have something positive to say. As critical as Keillor can be in his satirical writing, in the monologues he gives a message of hope and affirmation. One can see the importance of hope in "The Royal Family" when the assumption of royal blood changes one family's self-perception overnight. Grace Campbell and her children learn to hold their heads up high and become self-reliant—all because of the hope of eventual recognition.

Sometimes it takes a crisis to make people reevaluate their circumstances and be grateful for what they have. That happens to Clarence Bunsen in "Thanksgiving" when imaginary problems combine with real ones to cause him extreme anxiety. After Barbara Ann announces not an impending divorce but an impending baby, Clarence is overcome with joy. He tells her about setting off rockets when he found out Arlene was expecting her. He thinks about the chance people take when they have a baby. Everyone know babies come with no guarantees. One can only hope they will turn out all right, but Clarence concludes that producing a child is "a fine chance to take" (164).

It takes a different kind of crisis for Daryl Tollerud to reach his own feelings of affirmation. In his search for the letter his mother has mentioned to him, he finds long-kept pay stubs from his father's meager salary. He realizes his own frugality is a product of his upbringing. Then it occurs to him to wonder: what if one has been reared to face difficulties and disappointments and instead life gives everything wonderful? When he began his angry search for the letter, he was concerned about inheriting the farm. Now he realizes he has everything he could want—a wife he loves and six wonderful children. After expecting the worst, he has ended up with the best. All he has to do is appreciate the fact.

In "Lyle's Roof" the crisis has to do with self-esteem. Lyle berates himself for not being handy like his brother-in-law Carl. Lyle cannot accept himself, his strengths as well as his weaknesses, until he hears his daughter talk of the closeness of her family and the security that closeness has given her. Dwelling on his failings has kept Lyle from recognizing the many good qualities he has and the effect they have had on his family. His affirmation of self enables him to eliminate false pride and get the help he needs.

Keillor concludes "Hawaii" with a homily on love. Love is responsible for much of the affirmation in the monologues. Even though Lake Wobegon has its share of bickering couples, love seems to undergird their relationships. "Truckstop" and "Du, Du Liegst Mir in Herzen" end with declarations of devotion. Residents of Lake Wobegon seem able to forgive each other, making such declarations possible. In several discordant families, such as the Tollefsons and the Tolleruds, conflict between some members is offset by supportive love from others. Recognition of that love enables Daryl to conclude that "basically life is good" (91). Keillor echoes that feeling throughout the book.

ALTERNATE READING: FEMINIST CRITICISM

Men have long dominated the world of literature as both writers and critics. In the past so tight was their control that some women, like

George Eliot and the Brontë sisters, resorted to male pseudonyms to get their works published. Feminist criticism seeks to redress two situations that have resulted from male domination. One is the kind of recognition given to female writers, both those struggling for opportunities now and those ignored in the past. The other is the perpetuation of stereotypical gender assumptions and generalizations.

Feminists realize that much female talent has been stifled for want of an outlet. Thus they look for long-buried manuscripts and privately published work written by women long ago at the same time that they offer help to struggling contemporary writers. Even women writers who have achieved publication have usually had their works evaluated by male critics. Feminists are reevaluating such work. Frequently the result is a new appreciation of writers once dismissed as second rank.

When a writer is male, as is Garrison Keillor, the feminist critic must read his work from a woman's point of view. That sounds easy but sometimes it is not. Women were long trained to "read like men" (Lynn 18). Nevertheless, being aware of gender and actively looking for bias produces an awareness of stereotypes and assumptions when they appear. Sandra Gilbert notes, "Assumptions about the sexes . . . are entangled with some of the most fundamental assumptions Western culture makes about the very nature of culture" (33).

Perhaps Myrtle and Florian Krebsbach show most clearly some of those assumptions. Myrtle is what has traditionally been called a "battle-ax." She browbeats her rather timid husband, gets into a physical fight with her sister-in-law, and curses fluently. For his part, although he has his own faults, Florian is depicted as the long-suffering, put-upon husband who has to defend himself with wile and guile against his wife's machinations. People might find Myrtle's bossiness and abuse excessive in a man, but they laugh at those characteristics in a woman. Keillor is aware of that predictable reaction and uses Myrtle as a source of humor, but both she and Florian are stereotypes, nevertheless.

The relationship between Hjalmar Ingqvist and his daughter Corinne is also based on long-held assumptions. Hjalmar, a bank president, is a powerful male figure who has control of money, decisions, and by extension, his daughter's life. Corinne needs money to buy a house, but her father sees her as inept in the way she spends her money and the way she has chosen the house she wants. After berating and humiliating her, he writes her a personal check for $50,000, a seemingly magnanimous gesture that only serves to emphasize to Corinne that he is the one in control, the one with the authority, not she.

Many attitudes toward women can be traced back to the Middle Ages. The monastic tradition idealized the Virgin Mary but considered all other women *Eva Rediviva* or Eve reborn. Simone de Beauvoir has said that women in literature are depicted in much the same way, as either madonna or temptress. "David and Agnes, A Romance" indicates that these stereotypes still occur. Val Tollefson's father David left his mother and five children for another woman, Agnes Hedder. For forty years, Val has assumed that it was Agnes who lured David away. When he reads their letters, he realizes that it was the other way around. His willingness to accept the erroneous explanation for forty years reveals his belief in Agnes as temptress while ascribing to his mother, conveniently named Mary, the role of madonna.

Probably the most stereotypical paragraph in *Leaving Home* occurs in "Hawaii." Keillor says that when Lutheran women get to heaven "they'll think it's church and look for the stairs to go down to the basement, where the kitchen is" and "[w]hen the men arrive, they'll look at the Father's mansions and talk about siding: aluminum vs. cedar shakes" (218). The women, even in heaven, are consigned to the kitchen, or consign themselves there out of long tradition. They remain in a supportive role while men are depicted as the decision makers and the doers.

The fact that a writer shows stereotypical characters and stereotypical thinking by those characters does not necessarily mean that the writer holds those opinions. In Lake Wobegon Keillor presents a conservative small town with traditional beliefs, some of which he ridicules. He does not, however, balance the presentation with any strong women. Divorced women become more dependent than they were as housewives. Married women seem to be secondary in importance to their husbands. The few single women who have the intelligence and fortitude to change things have moved away. In story after story someone declares that life is good in Lake Wobegon. It is not surprising that those who so declare are all men.

6

We Are Still Married
(1989)

In his introduction to *We Are Still Married*, Garrison Keillor gives as a reason for the book: a need to show his audience that he did not become lazy when he quit his radio show and moved to Denmark. Although the seventy-six pieces collected here originally appeared in a variety of publications, sometimes under different titles or slightly altered, most were first published in the *New Yorker*. Some are signed contributions while twenty-one appeared in one of the regular columns.

Keillor has always considered himself a writer, not a radio personality, and he admits that it was difficult doing the radio show all those years. By the time this book came out, he was working again at the *New Yorker* and rejoicing "to be back among *paper*" (xvi). Even so, some of the stories and poems had their genesis on *A Prairie Home Companion*, his radio show.

The book is divided into five sections. On first glance, the reader assumes the pieces are grouped according to genre. "House Poems" is a collection of poetry and "Stories" does indeed contain stories. "Letters," however, contains nothing in letter format while "The Lake" is organized around the subject of Lake Wobegon and does have letters.

Nonetheless, organization is irrelevant to appreciation of the volume. Keillor's wit takes all forms here, and in this collection one can find something for every taste.

PLOT DEVELOPMENT

The first division of the book, entitled "Pieces," opens with "End of the Trail." In the middle of the twentieth century, cigarettes were omnipresent in all but ultraconservative locales. Sophisticates smoked; lowlifes smoked. Even the nonsmoking hostess was expected to provide ashtrays for her guests. That scene changed only gradually. As testing began to suggest that tobacco hurt not just the smoker but also those who inhaled secondhand smoke, public places began to set aside nonsmoking areas. People began to post "Thank you for not smoking" signs in their homes and offices. Even before whole buildings elected to become smoke free and employees huddled outside in the cold to take cigarette breaks, smokers were beginning to feel like pariahs. In "The End of the Trail" Keillor does what the good satirist always does: he takes the present situation one step further than it really is. In that one step, smokers move from being ostracized to being actually hunted down by federal agents. As agents close in on the hiding place of the last few holdouts, a mother scribbles messages to her children. The treatment of smokers as dangerous criminals is funny, but the piece also attests to the addictive hold smoking can have.

Keillor wrote "Three New Twins Join Club in Spring" shortly after the Minnesota Twins won the 1987 World Series. The Cardinals were predicted to take the series and were ahead three games to two after the first five games. However, the Twins won the last two, leading the narrator of this piece to gloat to some unnamed fan of another club. The narrator attributes the team's success to good works. The players have gone together to purchase a farm where they work alongside the juvenile delinquents they are trying to rehabilitate. Descriptions of players newly acquired in trades verge on tall tales, but Duane Mueller in particular should work well with a team that keeps in shape by chopping wood and carrying water. Duane developed his pitching arm by delivering papers and whipping cake mix for his mother. In addition, the Twins have just signed a recent high school graduate for a $1,200 bonus. He turned down millions to play with this team known for its "[p]ersonal character and loyalty and dedication" (10).

Even though the World Series was very exciting in 1987, and the Twins really did win, many baseball fans were beginning to become disenchanted with the sport in the 1980s. The million-dollar contracts and bonuses seemed out of proportion to the salaries of fans. The emphasis on personal selflessness here expresses a quality many fans found missing from the sport.

In "Your Book Saved My Life, Mister," Dusty Pages, a second-rate author of westerns, longs to hear someone tell him, "Your books have meant so much to me" (11). He plants himself near the western section of stores so he can be easily recognized. However, when people realize who he is, their usual response is "I thought so" (11). Chagrined that shoppers step by him to buy the work of competitors, Dusty concludes that his writing may be at fault. In one book he has the hero achieve great feats of derring-do to rescue the heroine only to tell her he is glad she is all right and ride on. He thinks he is being realistic, but he acknowledges that his readers might have expected something else. Finally Dusty encounters someone who tells him his book saved his life, but the details are not what Dusty expects to hear.

"Who We Were and What We Meant by It" takes aim at two different aspects of the world of art and entertainment. In May 1983 a Bulgarian artist named Christo made news by wrapping eleven islands in Biscayne Bay with pink plastic. The project cost $3 million even though it lasted only two weeks. Performance art many be transitory, but traditionally the visual arts have permanence. Thus the Christo project attracted many scoffers.

In this article written in 1984, Keillor takes a slap at outré artists at the same time that he makes fun of all who revere the haunts of the rich and famous. Elvis Presley fans go on pilgrimage to Graceland in Memphis while James Joyce fans retrace the steps of Leopold Bloom and Joyce himself in Dublin. In this story fans of Momentism, a sixties "happening" that turned into a movement, splash in a fountain and eat where the founders are said to have eaten. The narrator is one of the founders who is upset that fans are trying to imitate what was to have been for the moment only.

In "The Current Crisis in Remorse," Keillor makes fun of a society that allows criminal offenders to excuse their actions because of a variety of social ills. The narrator, a professional remorse officer, explains that the 1970s were a "regretless time" (23) when mass murderers blamed their actions on deep-fried foods and people defended theft and mayhem as appropriate responses to criticism. The narrator was not highly regarded by his peers until the public rose up in arms. Then City Hall tried to immediately implement remorse programs. However, it soon became apparent that what government really wanted was lip service to the idea without really making people feel sorry. By the end, the narrator has left his municipal job and gone to work for a Japanese company. The Japanese, he says, have a much more highly developed sense of guilt and reward him well.

"The People vs. Jim" is very short. A magazine writer named Jim is called on the carpet for writing list articles. Everything he produces seems to have numbers in it. He writes about the twenty best this and the fifty top that. He is being chastised by the editor for producing readers who now find it difficult to read anything that is not numbered. Because there really are people who seem unable to understand well-organized paragraphs if they lack numbers or bullets, Keillor is making a valid point. Perhaps the Jims of the world *are* at fault.

A composition perennially performed at youth concerts is Benjamin Britten's *The Young Person's Guide to the Orchestra*. It combines narration and music so that those just learning to appreciate orchestral music can understand what the instruments look like, how they sound, and how they are used in the orchestra. Britten used a theme by Henry Purcell to produce an instructive but very listenable piece. In a parody of *The Young Person's Guide*, Keillor has written "A Young Lutheran's Guide to the Orchestra." Young Lutherans, Keillor says, must ask several questions before they choose an instrument to play, among them whether a Lutheran even belongs in an orchestra. While organists and choir members can be sure their musical talent is a gift from God, Keillor warns young Lutherans that the Bible says nothing about orchestras; it never mentions that Christ played an instrument or went to concerts. Orchestras play for operas, which are filled with Mephistopheleses and pagan deities. Keillor asks, "Is that any place for a Christian?" (31).

A Lutheran who is determined to play despite such dangers must decide which instrument is best. The parallel to the Britten piece starts at this point as Keillor goes through the instruments one by one, pointing out their drawbacks and pitfalls from the viewpoint of a religious conservative. One instrument is inappropriate because it is too worldly, another too sensual, and still another, "a temptation to pride" (33). He finally concludes that there are only two instruments a Lutheran should consider: percussion of some sort or the harp. Having to count measures waiting to play their few notes teaches a percussionist patience while the harp's lack of mobility teaches humility. Both are good qualities for a Lutheran to have.

This is amusing as an essay, but an effective parody of music should be musical, and that is what the essay really is—a script written for performance with music composed by Randall Davidson. It was commissioned by the Minneapolis-based Plymouth Music Series and first performed in Seattle in 1988 (Scholl, *Garrison* 169). Available on both audio and video tapes, recorded versions are very popular with musicians, whether or not they are Keillor fans.

"Maybe You Can Too" spoofs media stories about people who, with seemingly no expertise, form profitable companies and get rich overnight. In a jab at country kitsch, the decorating trend that puts covers on toasters and aprons on brooms, he has one woman make millions by clothing computer screens in skirts. By the end it is clear that Keillor has a third target, the how-to-get-rich come-on. The narrator tells readers they too can find the secret to becoming wealthy by sending a mere $239.50.

"A Little Help" starts with a phone call from actor Richard Gere to the husband of an unappreciated wife and mother. The call is just one of many set up by Hollywood Calls, a group of movie stars who bypass the big charities and political campaigns for which stars were once lauded. Today's stars prefer the personal touch, eschewing the publicity of popular causes to try to make a difference on a one-to-one basis. Interestingly, an ordinary person turns the tables on one star and offers him the popular version of psychological support with surprising results.

"A Liberal Reaches for Her Whip" appeared in *Harper's* in January 1989 under the title "When You Kick a Liberal: A Post-Election Fable." The Democratic candidate in the 1988 Presidential election was Michael Dukakis, an unabashed liberal who supported gun control and opposed the death penalty. Conservatives considered those positions "soft on crime." They used a controversial ad about convict Willie Horton to play on people's fears and convince voters that Dukakis's views were dangerous. The result was a decisive victory for Republican George Bush.

The fable uses several examples. It starts with Aunt Hazel, a truly nice person who is maligned because she is too generous with her time and energy. People who could find something good in Hitler cannot believe the unending generosity of Hazel and accuse her of being selfish and egotistical. After a contemporary retelling of the Parable of the Prodigal Son, Keillor concludes that "jerks [are] rewarded, nice people abused" (48). That takes him to the real fable. Liberalism, an old woman, is pushed down the stairs by Presidents Reagan and Bush, who stand at the top and laugh at her. She forgives them as a good liberal should, but she rises lean and mean and looking for action.

Parade, a Sunday magazine supplement to many newspapers, carries a question and answer column about celebrities. When someone once asked about a Hollywood exposé by Mark Van Doren, the *Parade* columnist suggested that the questioner was confusing the poet, author, and critic with Mamie Van Doren, a starlet of the 1950s. Garrison Keillor uses this excerpt as a lead-in to "Hollywood in the Fifties." In it he puts together famous people with the same last names—swimming movie star Esther Williams, baseball slugger Ted Williams, poet William Carlos Williams, actress Vanessa Williams, and singer Andy Williams, for example—and concocts unlikely families in a ridiculous scenario around a Hollywood pool. What is not so ridiculous is the ending exodus of serious writers from the Hollywood scene.

Most people consider urban renewal a positive change that leaves little opportunity for ridicule, but when reclaimed neighborhoods become trendy, Keillor can find much to make fun of, including the names of shops like The Yarnery, The Phonery, and The Pottery Wottery. In "Lifestyle" he takes aim at the selfish, feel-good way of living seemingly sanctioned by the Reagan White House and popularized in the eighties by "yuppies," young urban professionals. Rob and Nancy Niles realize that the demands of their teenage children are taking all of their time and that they have no time to grow, individually or as a couple. They "choose not to accept that" (58) and solve the situation by selling their children. Everything seems to progress swimmingly until the stock market crash and a jogger's fall trigger the demise of the neighborhood. Keillor does not exaggerate reality in depicting the short-lived popularity of such areas. One of the characteristics of the eighties was the fickleness of the yuppies, who seemed in endless pursuit of the "in" places to live and spend their time and money.

Senator Dan Quayle of Indiana was elected vice president of the United States in November 1988. George Bush chose Quayle as his running mate because of his conservatism, but early in the election campaign it became apparent that Quayle was more of a liability to the ticket than an asset. Ill-advised remarks seemed to indicate a lack of intelligence, and his own past presented problems for a party trying to convince voters it was more patriotic than its Democratic opponents. Newspapers revealed that his father had used his influence to get Quayle into the Indiana National Guard so that he did not have to go to Vietnam. "He Didn't Go to Canada" appeared in the *New Yorker* immediately before the elections. In it Keillor makes no attempt to disguise his subject. He even names his protagonist Dan.

This Dan really wants to go to Vietnam but agrees to join the Indiana National Guard when his father arranges it. Guard members appear to have it easy, playing golf every day and partying at night, but in reality the Guard is the president's secret weapon. Soviet spy satellites think the golfers are just civilians taking it easy. They cannot see the command center housed in deep bunkers around the ninth hole. They do not recognize as military hardware the forklifts, portable toilets, bulk-milk trucks, and riding lawn mowers carefully stored in warehouses. Thus Dan spends his days, trying to bear the tension of knowing that his typewriter will switch to invisible ink if he types "Hoosier," that his cyanide capsule is hidden in a golf ball. Suddenly the war is over. For years members of the Guard suffer from "postwar regret" (69) because they got no opportunity to fight. Then Dan meets his former colonel, who tells him he should have no remorse. Instead, being proud that he did not go to Canada like others who avoided the draft, he should "[a]ccept the rewards of a grateful nation" (70).

"How the Savings and Loans were Saved" appeared in the *New Yorker* in October 1989, two months after President George Bush signed into law a bill providing for the biggest federal rescue in history, that of failed savings and loan companies. After deregulation in 1980, the savings and loan industry was plagued with fraud and mismanagement. Many saw the 1989 bailout as a way to get taxpayers to pay for the crimes and ineptitude of savings and loan managers. In this piece Keillor portrays them as Huns who, along with Goths, Visigoths, and other invading forces, take over the city of Chicago and camp in the savings and loan offices. During the ensuing crisis the president continues his daily activities while spouting platitudes. In the end he gets the Huns to go away by paying a ransom of $160 billion, the anticipated cost of the real bailout.

The second section of *We Are Still Married* is entitled "The Lake." Everything in it is related in some way to Lake Wobegon. The first article, "Letters from Jack," takes the form of letters written over a period of seven years by the owner of Jack's Auto Repair, one of the first fictional sponsors of Keillor's radio show, *A Prairie Home Companion*. The letters vary from complaints that the sponsorship has not brought in the business Jack hoped it would to comments that the show is boring. He says he understands that Keillor's religious beliefs consider entertainment immoral but asks that he compromise those beliefs enough to make the show at least interesting. He chides Keillor for all his "wheezing and chuffing" (79) during the news from the lake and suggests that he check the plumbing before he reopens the World Theater. In perhaps the best letter of the collection, Jack tells what it was like to attend the World back when more people played baseball and one could buy fresh fruit in theatre lobbies. The agility of an actor delivering a soliloquy was admirable, and "death speeches had a furtive, restless quality" (83) because the dying actor had to watch the audience in case he needed to take cover. Jack pans a television show Keillor did in 1986. He tells him that "thirty minutes of a man speaking in a fast Midwestern voice about guilt, death, the Christian faith, and small-town life is not what people look for in a stage performance" (85).

"Three Marriages" is also comprised of letters, each written by a traveler to someone back home. In the first Gladys Tollerud is writing to friends about the trip she and her husband Roy are taking to Texas. Gladys thinks back to visiting Roy when he was stationed in Texas in 1944. She recalls that they considered remaining in Texas and thinks that would have been fine. She realizes there is "a lot more to the world" (90) than what they are used to in Minnesota. However, Roy cannot remember ever discussing staying in Texas. He gets angry and suggests that she is unhappy with him, their family, and their life together. Gladys ends her letter with resignation.

Ruth and Bob Luger were married ten years ago and are now traveling to visit Bob's old buddies, friends he has not seen since the wedding. In a letter to her sister, Ruth describes stops in Rapid City, Las Vegas, and San Diego to visit people she would have nothing to do with if she were at home. She learns that even though she loves her husband, she finds him weak and does not like him very much. She concludes that God must have engineered this trip to educate her because it certainly is not enjoyable.

In the third letter Clarence Bunsen is writing to his wife Arlene from Saskatchewan, where he is ice fishing. Because ice fishing takes no skill, it leaves time for "the religious aspect of fishing" (95). In Clarence's case that aspect is the contemplation of his sins. He confesses dawdling when he should have hurried to help her with sick children, ignoble behavior when a squirrel robbed the bird feeder, and jealousy when Arlene received a Christmas card from a high school sweetheart. Thinking about it years later, Clarence realizes he is still jealous, and he cannot wait to get home to Arlene. None of the writers seem to be enjoying their trips away from home, but all, despite very different marital relationships, seem to have learned something from the experience.

"Babe" is a rumination about sports in Lake Wobegon. Winning teams have been hard to come by in that town. In fact, some fans have wondered whether local players "are suffering from a Christian upbringing that stresses . . . unworthiness" (100). When a team gets a good lead, the players seem to feel sorry for their opponents and let them catch up. The losing ways are not confined to the Whippets, the local baseball team, but can be found in football and basketball as well. In fact, one has to go back to the 1940s to find the Golden Age of local sports.

Then the baseball team was the Lake Wobegon Schroeders, brothers who were managed by their father, E. J. Shroeder. E. J. was never satisfied with their performance even though his sons were extraordinary players, so good in fact that they played Babe Ruth and the Sorbosal All-Stars when they came to town. The Babe was dying of cancer and so ill that he had to be helped to stand. Nevertheless, he did bat, and the results were something people still speak of in awe.

"How I Came to Give the Memorial Day Address" is the first of the pieces in *We Are Still Married* that can be considered a story. It concerns acceptance of social responsibility, in this case the chairmanship of the Memorial Day celebration and arrangement for an appropriate speaker. The task keeps being handed off from one person to another. Clarence Bunsen asks his brother Clint, who gives the task to Clifford Turnblad, who relays it to Arlene Bunsen, who passes it on to Judy Ingqvist, who solicits Val Tollefson for the job. Keillor combines an anecdote or characterization with each of the shifts. By the end, Val asks the narrator, in town for a short visit, to give the Memorial Day speech. On such short notice, it is not a memorable speech, but Clint tells him the good thing is that "it's all over" (130). And indeed that seems to be the point. Once the speech is given, school can end, baseball can start, and sweet corn will appear.

"Who Do You Think You Are?" begins as a meditation on the effectiveness of the line Keillor used to open the monologue portion of his radio show: "It has been a quiet week in Lake Wobegon, my hometown." One of its problems, he admits, is that he could not readily go from that line into talk of "dreams of boundless grandeur" (133), but neither does life in Lake Wobegon lend itself to the discussion of dreams. Any mention is apt to invoke the line, "Who do you think you are?" (135). The piece is divided into segments by "Hey," an experimental come-on for locations not Lake Wobegon. These are highly personal reminiscences about growing up, rejection, and desire for success while always expecting the put-down of the title.

Keillor says the third section of the book contains letters written from 1982 to 1988. However, "Letters" really contains essays on a variety of subjects, none of them in letter form. "How to Write a Letter" and "Postcards," although not really process essays, suggest ways to keep in touch effectively. "Sneezes" and "Hoppers" classify people, and "Subway" and "Stinson Beach" are primarily descriptive.

Some of the essays use personal examples but are general in nature while others are responses to specific experiences, occasionally from long ago. "Estate" draws on a brief stint as a member of the fourth estate, when Keillor was assigned to write obituaries for a St. Paul paper. Taking his job seriously, he put in all the accomplishments the family requested although the editor refused to let him mention one woman's rhubarb cake. From that account he moves to estate sales he has attended. He hopes people will buy and appreciate his own things when he is gone.

"Laying on Our Backs Looking Up at the Stars" takes its title from *Huckleberry Finn* and recalls a time in 1971 when Keillor and a few friends left a party where everyone was discussing Vietnam, racial hatred, and despair. They tried to get perspective by lying on their backs and looking at the stars. Other essays start with more recent events: his son's return from a trip to Europe, his being asked to drop the puck for a hockey game, or his being voted one of the ten sexiest men in America by *Playgirl*. An engine explosion on a flight from Copenhagen leads to "Regrets," an introspective look at things Keillor wishes he had or had not done, and a trip with his second wife and their combined children provides the background for "Family Honeymoon."

Although Copenhagen is the setting for "Episcopal" and "Nu Er Der Jul Igen," most of the essays were written in New York City and deal with encounters and events there. Some are just musings prompted by something he has seen or read. "The Pennsylvania Dept. Of Agr." starts with a food label and moves to the desire for guarantees. In "Snowstorm" storm warnings cause him to contemplate the communal effect of a storm.

All thirty-six essays in "Letters" contain an idea on which Keillor expounds. The result may be a long narrative like "Country Golf" or less than a page like "Lutheran Pie." What they have in common is a personal glimpse into his world.

"House Poems" is a collection of ten poems, some serious, some humorous. Two are occasional poems, that is, poems written for a specific event. Keillor wrote "In Memory of Our Cat, Ralph" when the cat died and "On Becoming a Doctor" when Gettysburg College conferred on him the Doctor of Literature degree. Of the serious poems, "Mother's Poem" is perhaps the most successful. Its beginning captures completely the overworked, unappreciated mother's situation. In order to care for her husband and four children, she rises before dawn, the daylight hours providing insufficient time for her to meet the expectations of her family. She figures out that negligence on her part is a way to make herself appreciated, but her clever ploy does not diminish the enormity of her responsibility.

Several of the poems are humorous and employ the kind of near rhyme for which poet Ogden Nash is famous. Keillor focuses "Mrs. Sullivan" (273) on a quote by her architect husband, Louis Sullivan, who inspired the world of contemporary design with his famous statement— "Form follows function." In brief, sharp lines Keillor gives credit for the theory to Mrs. Sullivan. "The Solo Sock" (271–72) uses longer lines but still tries some Nashlike techniques by making up a near rhyme for *water*. In response to the idea that someone has stolen the mates for his socks, the speaker asks, "Why would they take one and not take the odder?" (11–12).

The final section is called "Stories." The first, "Meeting Famous People," pits a singer-songwriter named Sweet Brian against Big Tim Bowers, who considers himself Brian's biggest fan. When he spots Brian in an airport, he greets him so enthusiastically that Brian runs away. Tim pursues him through every kind of barrier, finally catching and hugging him. Thoroughly panicked, Brian calls Tim a vampire, slaps him, and writes "Your Biggest Fan," a derogatory song about him. Two years later the tables are turned. Tim, having successfully sued Brian, is now a big success, and Brian is dead. Keillor concludes with advice on how fans should conduct themselves when they meet famous people.

"The Lover of Invention" is broad humor about a caveman who, having invented a perfect cube, invents the wheel. The problem is that no one knows what to do with it. There is a conflict over a girl named Verne, and Charley, the inventor, leaves, hoping she will follow. She does not.

"Lonely Boy" could be an episode out of any lonely boy's summer. He meets a girl at the beach and falls for her. In attempts to impress her, he gives her a false name, has her drop him at a false home, and prepares a false family history. By the first date he is so exhausted by the lies, even the ones he has not had to tell, that when she asks what he is doing that summer, he tells her the truth. He tells her he works for the zoo. She takes umbrage at the thought of caged animals, and that is the end of the relationship. It is clear at the end of the story that the protagonist's internal conflict is in no way resolved. He berates himself for her departure, convinced that she would have fallen in love with him in time.

His attempt to think of what to say to bring her back ignores the fact that any relationship would be based on fabrication, not reality.

The protagonist of "What Did We Do Wrong?" is the first woman to break into major league baseball. Annie Szemanski has fewer problems with the game and her fellow players than she does with fans, sports writers, and support groups. She is the public relations director's nightmare. When he tells her the fans want to like her and begs her to make some gesture, she blows her nose. The gesture she finally makes, unfortunately on television, alienates fans and gets her a suspension and fine. Annie refuses to pay and simply disappears. By refusing to compromise in her confrontation with the external world of baseball, she retains her integrity but loses her profession.

An old song begins "My name is Yon Yonson, I come from Wisconsin, I work in a lumber mill there." Keillor uses the song at the beginning of "Yon" and then writes a story about him. This Yon leaves his lumber mill to go to live with his sister in New York City. He finds a job delivering flowers and goes on to open his own delivery business. By the end he is living comfortably in Connecticut where his answering machine recycles part of the song. There is no conflict in this story. Instead it is a fable in which Keillor points out that it is possible to leave the Midwest and be happy.

"The Art of Self-Defense" is about Ed, an ordinary man who is slow to anger. After the third baseman on his team is unnecessarily roughed up by a runner, he becomes angry at himself for not exploding at the time. He considers his tendency to avoid trouble a weakness. The more he thinks about it, the more he convinces himself that those who stay away from physical conflict eventually do something terrible: they order the bombing of remote villages or wipe out Indian tribes. Thus begins his attempt to hit someone to avoid committing an unspeakable act later on. He gets off a bus in a bad neighborhood expecting to be accosted by ruffians, but the only ones who come up to him are panhandlers. When he finally has a confrontation, it occurs when and where he least expects it. Nevertheless, Ed decks the man, and his internal quandary is resolved.

"End of an Era" is not a story but a morality tale. It marks the end of Larry, a former hippie who dies suddenly while cleaning out the garage. Among his effects is a will requesting that his funeral be a "Celebration of Life." Although the celebration idea is not extreme, his specific requests—that his ashes be mailed to hundreds of people he admired, that motorists be stopped and invited to the funeral—are too excessive to be carried out. The woman with whom he currently lives thinks it appropriate that he dies "trying to get [his] life out from under the debris" (347). The sad thing is that once the junk from the garage deck is carted off, there is nothing left of Larry.

"Glasnost" starts with a July 1988 article from the *Washington Post* concerning *glasnost*, the new Russian openness. The speaker is Leonid, a Kiev cabdriver who uses the idea of *glasnost* to try to seduce the women who ride in his cab. Claiming that he was open before Gorbachev, he tells the women that they need to be "open" too. This is not a story but a creative line.

"After a Fall" is included in *Happy to Be Here* and has been discussed in connection with that book. The next story, "My Life in Prison," takes a personal experience and builds on it. Starting with fighting siblings who are apt to be punished even when they are innocent, the speaker moves on to talk of trespasses that go unpunished. He remembers hitting his cousin with a pair of stilts. The cousin calmly told him he would go to prison some day, and the speaker has been waiting ever since. He expects at any time to be plucked up and put down behind bars with a sentence of 512 years. Such is the effect guilt can have on a person.

The final story is the title piece, "We Are Still Married." It is a media spoof that starts with reporters coming to live with a couple when their dog is dying. The dog recovers but the marriage barely survives the prying and publicity as the wife finds an eager audience for charges that her husband is a cold, uncaring slob.

CHARACTER DEVELOPMENT

Because very few of the pieces in this collection are what can be considered short stories, very few have traditional plots. Likewise few have traditional characters. It is possible to analyze two that do, however.

One such is the protagonist in "Lonely Boy." The boy is more than lonely; he has a serious identity problem. Fittingly, Keillor gives only his last name, Wiscnek. For most of the story he goes by a name he makes up, Ryan Tremaine.

When the boy meets Rhonda at the beach, his first action is to dive into the water after her even though he has never dived before. The difference between the two young people is apparent from the beginning. She has the skills that come from having leisure time, opportunity, and money. Lacking those skills, he has only chutzpah. Nevertheless, his dive is successful, and that success emboldens him enough to pursue her.

The boy's awareness of class differences, evident in his reluctance to tell her his real name, becomes acute when she invites him over and he cannot find her house in the maze of lanes and drives and carefully unmarked driveways that characterize her part of town. Yet rather than discouraging him, this gulf only spurs him to work harder. He researches the college she plans to attend so that he can say he already goes there. He tries to get information on someone's cousin, for whom Rhonda originally mistook him. He works out a whole scenario about his parents' dying in a plane crash in case he has to explain why she cannot meet his parents.

The boy considers Ryan, the character he creates, superior to himself, "more worthy of her love" (314). In a very complicated rationalization he decides that her love could eventually turn him into the better character he has to fake being in order to get her to love him.

All the arduous plotting and attempts to keep story lines straight are useless when he tells her about the zoo, but the boy sees that as his only mistake and chastises himself for revealing that one true fact about himself. At the end he remains in his dream world, assuming that they would have married had he not ruined the relationship with honesty.

Another character is Annie Szemanski, the baseball player. Although her performance at bat and in the field is exemplary, Annie cannot handle other aspects of fame. She underestimates the importance of fans and reporters, who together precipitate her failure.

When she first arrives from Bolivia, she talks freely to reporters. She discusses the difficulties of being a woman in a man's sport and explains that she began to chew tobacco because "no matter how bad anybody treats you, it's not as bad as this" (317). Fans start out being very supportive. They wear Annie caps and wave Annie flags and are only somewhat put off by the stains of tobacco juice on her chin and uniform. The first critical press article is mild, condemning *all* players for the disgusting habit of tobacco chewing.

However, when other aspects of her conduct begin to imitate those of male players, Annie becomes an increasingly controversial figure with both the fans and the press. She gets thrown out of a game for swearing at the umpire and fighting on the field. That leads the League of Women Voters and other groups to get involved, stating their approval of Annie as a model "for all women who are made to suffer guilt for their aggressiveness" (319). Although a dropped pop fly garners only a few boos from the stands, she yells something unprintable at the crowd. That is the point at which the press weighs in. A writer, frustrated by years in the Lifestyles section of the paper, uses this instance to voice her personal acrimony. In headlines she declares that Annie blames the boos on "sexual inadequacy" (319) of the fans.

Things come to a head on a road trip when Annie hits a home run and refuses to acknowledge the cheering crowd. In a later interview she indicates that she has no intention of fulfilling the expectations of fans. When the manager suggests that she owes them the opportunity to have pictures taken with her, she is incensed. She feels no obligation to her fans and cares nothing about tradition. She is equally uncaring about her relationship with the press. She tells reporters they are out of shape, and she turns down Joe Garagiola when he requests a pregame interview.

Although the pressures on Annie come from without, her own inability to compromise causes her downfall. She believes that playing well should be enough, but in a game that the nation claims as its own, players are judged as much on their handling of the public as they are on handling of a baseball. Annie cannot accept that and opts to leave the game.

THEMATIC ISSUES

Garrison Keillor uses many themes in this broad collection, but one that recurs many times concerns political liberalism. In the introduction, he enumerates all the presidents he can remember and says he became a Democrat at age eighteen. He finds perplexing the popularity of Ronald Reagan and the unpopularity of Jimmy Carter, whom he considered a man of integrity. Although the words "conservative" and "liberal" are relative terms, Keillor uses them here as they tended to be used in the 1980s. He considers liberal those people who have a social conscience, who "carry water for a million good causes" (49). Liberals, he maintains, are those who were taught to take turns, to share, and to feel guilty when they were selfish. He sees no such guilt in the 1980s.

Keillor uses several pieces to voice sorrow at the state of the nation. In "A Liberal Reaches for Her Whip," he portrays liberalism, with its concerns for minorities, the poor, and the helpless, as an old woman kicked into the cellar by Presidents Bush and Reagan. Indeed, Reaganomics, as President Reagan's economic program was popularly called, tried to cut everything from school lunch programs, which affected most public school students, to welfare programs, which affected the young, the old, and those with the greatest needs. At the same time that Reaganomics took away support from those most vulnerable, it cut taxes on both corporations and individuals and increased funding for defense and programs that helped business. The result was a tripling of the national debt while Reagan was president.

In "A Liberal Reaches for Her Whip" Keillor draws a parallel between the prodigal son in the biblical parable and the wastrels who seem to have their improvidence rewarded by Republicans. The biggest reward for waste and irresponsibility was the savings and loan bailout, which he attacks in "How the Savings and Loans Were Saved." In "Reagan," he criticizes the campaign of George Bush, Reagan's Republican successor, for using racism rather than trying to eliminate it. He does not in any way accuse Bush himself of being a racist, but the racist overtones of the Willie Horton ads used by the Bush campaign were well known.

In addition, in the poem "Guilt and Shame," the protagonist is a clear personification of the Reagan-Bush attitudes. Not only does the protagonist ignore the needs of his father, mother, and child, but he refuses to feel guilty for ignoring them. Instead, he proclaims that everything is wonderful. It takes a cat to change his outlook.

Another theme Keillor uses is an indictment of self-indulgence. He handles it in a lighthearted way in the poem "Obedience," which tells of a boy who defies every instruction his mother gives him just for the pleasure of wallowing in disobedience. Keillor gives a good reason to postpose some sins till adulthood: they will be more fun when he is older.

Keillor's objective is always humor, but his condemnation of self-indulgence in the stories is serious, particularly when people rationalize their behavior by spouting popular psychology. Thus in "Lifestyles" Rob and Nancy complain that keeping up with their two teenagers is hurting their marital relationship. They claim they have no choice but to do what is best for themselves. That is why they feel obligated to sell their children.

"The Current Crisis in Remorse" centers not around remorse but around its absence. From the murder suspect who tries to convince a social worker he is really "a caring type of guy" (23) to the person who expects vile actions to be excused because he had a "particularly upsetting life-experience" (24), people do not say they are sorry. Instead they assume they can do whatever they feel like doing and then explain it away with no consequences. Keillor finds that reprehensible.

ALTERNATE READING: BIOGRAPHICAL AND
HISTORICAL CRITICISM

Writers often create protagonists very different from themselves. Even a first-person narrator may have gender or ideology different from that of the author. Nevertheless, effective writers do draw on experience as well as on observation, and sometimes a biographical reading is warranted. Biographical criticism insists that knowing something about the author is important. Closely aligned to biographical criticism is historical criticism, which holds that setting is also meaningful. Events taking place at a certain time and in a certain place can influence what a writer writes and how he presents it. Many pieces in *We Are Still Married* openly refer to people, institutions, and events, but biographical or historical criticism can be applied to pieces that do not.

Keillor's well-known aversion to television comes out in several places. In "Letters from Jack," Jack tells Keillor he is aiming for disaster by televising his show. He says it will be so terrible that television is the only appropriate place for it. Jack maintains that radio is superior because it is "the medium of imagination" (84). In "We Are Still Married" Willa, the wife who tells the world about her uncaring husband, is featured on several daytime news and talk shows and finally on the nightly news on ABC. Keillor's personal attitude about the insipid quality of most television shows is apparent.

Another concern of Keillor's is the intrusive quality of much of today's media. When Keillor left Minnesota, he felt that he had been hounded by the press. He mourned his loss of privacy. His animus toward the press comes out in several fictional episodes here. In "How I Came to Give the Memorial Day Address," Keillor hypothesizes an explosion with predatory reporters covering it. Oblivious to human suffering, they concentrate on getting newsworthy pictures with a red wagon or a dollhouse on top of the debris. In a scornful complaint about God, the narrator exclaims, "[W]e despair and He sends the press" (119). Equally telling is the picture of the *People* magazine reporters who move in with Earl and Willa in "We Are Still Married." Supposedly writing an article about the dying dog, in reality the reporters pry into every facet of Earl and Willa's private lives, eventually causing crisis in their marriage.

The ultimate indication of Keillor's attitude toward the press comes in "My Life in Prison," a fictionalized story about himself written originally for a November 1988 issue of the *Atlantic*. In it, when he tells a reporter that the worst thing his parents ever did to him was punish him unfairly, the reporter writes that he is bitter toward his old mother. What appears as *Geek: An Unauthorized Biography of You Know Who (The Big Jerk)* is a reference to an unauthorized biography by Michael Fedo, and an article about a poor, sick boy whom Keillor is supposed to have disappointed is an exaggeration of articles that appeared about the time he left Minnesota. Nevertheless, the fact that he can make fun of writers and reporters indicates that Keillor's anger has subsided, and he is able to see the humor in the way celebrities become fair game on which the media feeds.

Historical elements in Keillor's fiction are as recognizable as biographical elements. Like any good commentator on the contemporary scene, Keillor is able to detect silliness in popular culture, and he exploits that silliness for his own ends. That is the case in "Who We Were and What We Meant by It." In that story he ridicules the fringes of the art world, personified by Christo and his highly publicized island wrapping. He also makes fun of the cultlike followings of public personalities, as well as those who try to create movements where there are none. Other echoes of the popular scene in the 1980s can be found in "Lifestyle" and "End of the Trail." One would have difficulty understanding both of these outside of their historical context.

Biographical and historical readings are not always warranted, but when they are, both can add depth to one's understanding of literature. Such is the case with several pieces in this collection.

7

WLT: A Radio Romance
(1991)

For his fifth book, Garrison Keillor returns to a series of short stories he wrote for his first. Most of the pieces collected in that first book, *Happy to Be Here*, are unconnected parodies, satires, or tales, but four of them use the theme of an early radio station, its founding, its stars, and its shows. Keillor takes those four stories, modifies them, and builds on them to create *WLT: A Radio Romance*.

The original four stories start with "WLT (The Edgar Era)" and explain the origin of the radio station. The Edgar brothers initially try broadcasting as a merchandising ploy for their restaurant. According to regulations of the Federal Communications Commission, the call letters of all radio stations are supposed to begin with the letters *W* or *K*, depending on whether their transmitters are located east or west of the Mississippi River. The Edgars take advantage of that rule and give their call letters a double meaning: because theirs is a sandwich restaurant, they call the station WLT, standing for "with lettuce and tomato." The three other early stories, named for WLT's most popular shows, are "The Slim Graves Show," "Friendly Neighbor," and "The Tip-top Club."

The seeds from which *WLT: A Radio Romance* emerges are those four early stories, but Keillor feels no obligation to use the same characters and situations he created ten or more years earlier and just extend them. Instead he changes names and personalities. He expands themes and settings. In particular, he changes tone.

Because *WLT* is a novel, Keillor can create more fully developed characters and a more complicated plot. He can more intricately link characters and plot so that each affects the other. Nevertheless, the fact that the novel genre affords those opportunities does not mean Keillor will take advantage of them. In *Lake Wobegon Days*, the only one of his previous books that is not a collection of short works, he does not. Instead he creates loosely connected characters and stories in episodes that are organized around the seasons. Although some reviewers called it a novel, it lacks a novel's centrality. *WLT: A Radio Romance* is a novel, however, and for the first time Keillor gives his readers a long fiction work with characters who develop and change, with both conflicts and subconflicts, and with multiple themes.

Keillor's objectives in writing *WLT* seem to be contradictory. On the one hand, he pays tribute to radio by presenting its history. He makes no attempt to document actual historical events, but instead fictionalizes the way the medium developed in cities across the United States. Entrepreneurs like the Soderbjergs used both luck and foresight to bring about an entertainment revolution that continues today. On the other hand, the tone of this novel is dark, leading some critics to accuse Keillor of deliberately writing about undesirable characters and events to offset earlier accusations of appealing to nostalgia. Whether or not that was his goal, he certainly cannot be accused of any sentimentality in this novel.

PLOT DEVELOPMENT

WLT: A Radio Romance opens with the Soderbjerg brothers, like their Edgar predecessors, experimenting with the new phenomenon, radio, as a means of attracting customers to their restaurant. Unlike the Edgars, they quickly leave the restaurant behind and concentrate on promoting the new station. At least Ray does. The other brother, Roy, is a dreamer who retreats to a farm and leaves his son to work with Ray in building the station. Ray and Roy Jr. complement each other, and the station prospers beyond their greatest hopes for it.

The central plot revolves around the station, its challenges, and its triumphs as it progresses from an advertising ploy to a full-blown commercial venture. Although later the Soderbjergs cannot agree on who had the idea for the initial broadcast on April 6, 1926, they do concur that it is a success. Lasting only forty-five minutes, that first broadcast combines jokes, poetry, and songs, all held together by running patter from Ray's lodge brother, who acts as master of ceremonies. Despite a celebratory reception after termination of the broadcast, no one is really sure anyone has heard it until Ray goes home and his wife Vesta tells him the broadcast came through as clearly as if the studio were in the next room. Vesta is impressed with the quality of the sound but not with the quality of the content, and she suggests ways to improve the latter.

The next day the broadcast is twice as long, partly because Vesta is reciting "better" poetry—William Wordsworth's "Intimations of Immortality" and William Cullen Bryant's "Thanatopsis"—and partly because some of Ray's friends offer to help with the broadcast. They sing, recite, and do animal imitations. By the third day so many people come to the restaurant to get on the air that serving food becomes impossible, and the Soderbjergs close the kitchen. A day later, when people hoping to get on the air start lining up at 9:00 A.M., "it is clear that Minneapolis [is] wild about radio" (23).

In no time the Soderbjergs expand the broadcast schedule to six hours a day, then twelve, then nineteen. The format includes regularly scheduled programs ranging from *Organ Reflections* and *Scripture Nuggets* to *The Classroom of the Air* and *The Farm Hour*. Nevertheless, by the end of a year Ray is depressed. Reopening the restaurant as a hamburger shop has made it very profitable, yet the patrons it attracts are not the Pillsburys but shoppers, retired people, and others who for some reason have free time in the middle of the day. The radio station, like the restaurant, is not attracting quality nor is it producing it. At one point, Ray even says he hopes people are not actually listening to the broadcast. He realizes that in one year the station has "broadcast more words than Shakespeare ever wrote," most of it "rat droppings" (29).

In his disgust he talks of selling the station and discusses the possibility with his sister Lottie, who owns 20 percent to the 40 percent of each brother. Because Lottie has had a falling out with Roy, she commits her share to Ray even though she does not understand what is going on. From that point on, Ray has control of the station. Although Roy Jr. runs the day-to-day operations, Ray makes all major decisions.

In addition to the prospect of selling, Ray discusses becoming an affiliate of the Columbia Broadcasting System. The New York agent who comes to Minneapolis to negotiate the contract, however, is so condescending that he insults Ray. Instead of selling or affiliating, Ray borrows money and boosts the wattage of the station. He also makes the decision to accept advertising. Vesta, a minister's daughter who now considers radio her mission, is incensed. She has hoped to use radio to uplift and educate people while Ray himself is apprehensive, wondering whether blatant advertising will be considered vulgar and alienate his audience. He need not have worried. Potential advertisers beg the station to take their money. Every time the station raises the rates, more advertisers show up, aware that radio publicity means the difference between success and failure in their own businesses.

Radio seems unaffected by the stock market crash of 1929, and within five years of its inception, WLT has become a gold mine for its owners. Still disturbed by what he sees as the "sheer trashiness of radio" (50), Ray nevertheless makes all the right business decisions. He sells the restaurant and moves the station into several floors of the Ogden Hotel where there is room to grow. Roy comes into town to protest, but he can do nothing, and he returns to the country to spend his time inventing things no one will ever use.

As Keillor continues to describe the station's meteoric rise, he devotes chapters to the first programs and the performers who become their first stars. He also begins a subplot that starts independently and only later ties in with the activities of the station. The subplot is the story of Francis With, a ten-year-old radio listener from Mindren, North Dakota. Francis writes a fan letter to Little Becky, a character on *Friendly Neighbor*, but rather than mail it, he takes it with him when he travels to Minneapolis to tour WLT at the invitation of his Uncle Art, who works at the station. When Francis returns home, the focus of the novel returns with him. Francis's father, an engineer on the Great Northern Railroad, is killed in a train wreck, and Francis's life is immediately changed. His mother is unable to cope with the loss, and the family's life together slowly disintegrates. As their mother has a nervous breakdown and Francis argues with his sister Jodie, it seems that the only friendly voices in the house are those on the radio, particularly those of the Bensons on *Friendly Neighbor*. Eventually Jodie goes to live with their Aunt Emma and Uncle Charles, and Francis is left alone with his ailing mother. Even when Aunt Emma brings food, Jodie declines to come along, and Francis feels all connection with his sister severed except when he knows he and she are both listening to the same radio program. Meanwhile Francis's mother now spends her days in bed and listens to the radio all day long.

Francis lives a lonely existence, at school as well as at home. In the wreck that killed his father, a burst boiler literally cooked the crew. Classmates make up a cruel song about the death and taunt Francis with it until he astounds them by singing the song with them. That act gains him access to a clubhouse and school friends, but at the cost of disloyalty to his father.

Soon his mother is hospitalized, and Francis is taken to Minneapolis to live with Art and his wife Clare. Art has always been Francis's favorite uncle. When Francis was small, Art would tell jokes and do magic tricks to entertain him. However, Art does not bother to be on stage in his own home. He prefers to smoke, drink, and worry about Hitler. He rebuffs Francis when the boy attempts any conversation. For six years Francis lives with Art and Clare except for the times when they send him to stay in the crowded home of another relative. Francis is so miserable there that he always sneaks back to Art's and hopes that no one will notice that he has returned.

Francis's connection with WLT begins during his high school years when he starts to hang around the station and catch a ride home with Art. He plans to say he is researching a school paper if anyone asks why he is there, but no one ever does. He quickly realizes that people pay no attention to him, and he is able to observe the inner workings of the station, see all the wrangles, overhear all the gossip. He becomes an invisible fixture of the Green Room, the place where the actors gather before and after their shows. Some of the characters to whom he has been listening for years are just as he has imagined them, but Marjery, who plays Little Becky, is definitely not. She is a foul-mouthed teenager who smokes Camels and enjoys playing tricks on people. She is the one person who notices Francis. She gooses him, and when he bloodies her nose as she goes for him again, he earns the admiration of all the adults in the room. The next day one actor gives him a cup labeled "The Man Who Handled the Monster" (143).

After graduation, when he is voted "Most Anonymous Person in the Class of 1947" (171), Francis returns to Mindren to escape a polio epidemic. The town seems dead compared to Minneapolis, but while he is there he receives a letter offering him a college scholarship from the Hill Trust for Railroad Orphans. Although Francis considers the offer, his high school experience has been one of doing what he was told and waiting "for nothing to happen" (171). He figures that college will be more of the same, a place where someone else will date the beautiful girls and he will not fit in.

At the same time that Francis decides to decline the scholarship, he makes another important decision: he elects to change his name. In high school he was humiliated when a heartless student lisped into the public address system, "Oh Franthith With, Mithter Franthith With!" (170). He concludes that his problem is the "soft" ending of his last name. Thus he adds an *e*, rearranges the letters, and becomes White, Frank White. He thinks the names produce "a nice click like closing the bolt on a .22" (175).

Frank's life in Mindren ends when the neglected family home is sold for debts and his Aunt Emma takes his mother to a mental hospital. Collecting a few family mementos, Frank returns to Minneapolis. Art gives him $200, makes arrangements for a job interview at WLT, and tells him to get a room at the Antwerp, where many WLT employees stay. Frank is now on his own.

From this point on, the plot lines of WLT and Frank merge. Frank is hired as an errand boy for the Soderbjergs. His job is really to anticipate Ray's needs and listen when Roy Jr. feels loquacious. He also sends greeting cards, gives studio tours, and introduces guests by repeating their names loudly because the Soderbjergs can never remember anyone's name. Frank keeps a notebook in which he writes down every bit of information he learns about the station and the people who work there. Gradually he makes himself indispensable to the daily routine of WLT. Then when a transmitter goes out while Ray and Roy, Jr. are gone, Frank is the only one who will take responsibility for getting it fixed, and he becomes a hero.

Gradually Sloan, the man who hired Frank, gives him more and more of his own work to do until Frank is doing it all. That accomplishment does not go unnoticed by Roy Jr. He fires Sloan, who curses Frank and calls him an opportunist. Frank has worked hard to earn the trust of those around him, but this experience makes him tell himself not to stay in radio very long and to be sure to keep his eyes open.

When Maria Antonio, a young actress from Milwaukee, is hired, Frank meets her and falls in love. Determined to become more than an errand boy, he tells Maria he is going to ask Roy Jr. for a real job. However, before he gets the opportunity, Roy Jr. asks him what he thinks of baseball. Even though Frank is bored by the game and has planned to spend his evenings with Maria, he agrees to spend the next few weeks sitting in the press box with Buck Steller, The Voice of the Millers, and see what is going on. Roy Jr. thinks Buck is betting on the games, and he wants to be sure there is no repeat of the Black Sox scandal in Minneapolis. With Frank's powers of observation and attention to detail, Roy thinks he will be a perfect spy.

As it turns out, Frank uncovers no betting on the part of Buck, an announcer who is so blind that he has to make up many of the details that he cannot see. In embroidering the home games he actually attends, he calls into play the same talent he must use for away games. Then the basic information comes into the studio by ticker tape, and the announcer makes up the details. A tape reading *"Ball 3–2"* Buck transforms into "And McPherson is ready. He glares over at Reedy on third . . . and now he winds up, and throws a high inside fastball that sends Husik sprawling in the dirt. He jumps up! It looks as if he may charge the mound! But he thinks better of it, and steps back into the box. Three balls, two strikes" (259). In this way Keillor documents a valid part of early radio. It is well known that Ronald Reagan did such broadcasts when he was young. Keillor explains how it was done at the same time that he captures the feeling of press box competition between radio announcers and newspaper writers.

Having done Roy Jr.'s bidding by checking out the sportscaster, Frank deserves a chance at announcing, something he would really like to try. Nevertheless, when he asks for the opportunity, Roy Jr. tells him he is "too valuable to waste" (265). Not to be thwarted, Frank goes to the head announcer, Reed Seymour, and takes him out for beer. By the end of the second pitcher, Frank has secured an opportunity to go on the air for a couple of hours the next week. Knowing that Frank always likes to be active, Roy Jr. thinks he will be bored doing the announcing, but for Frank the idea of reaching all those people over the air far outweighs the negative prospect of inactivity. When his day finally comes, Frank does the livestock report, a public service announcement, and ads as well as introducing the programs. Even Roy Jr. has to admit he is a natural. It seems that Frank is on his way to a career as a radio personality.

From the beginning Keillor includes chapters on the sexual nature of everything from the surroundings of the station to the exploits of the owners and actors. The first chapter, "Studio B," explains why one of the station's three studios is the object of superstition. Before the station moved to the Ogden Hotel, Studio B was a bar with frescos of nude women. Although the frescos were papered over before the room became a studio, when some of the paper began to peel, employees peeled more. They eventually uncovered most of a woman whom they named Donna LaDonna. Now they consider it good luck to pat her in strategic places.

Most of the superstition connected with the room is not so positive, however. It is said to be haunted by the ghost of an announcer who lost his voice when broadcasting from the room. The ghost is blamed for the curse that hangs over the studio although the mishaps that occur are really due to tricks some actors play on others. Because all shows are broadcast live, making an actor do anything untoward is a sure way to cause embarrassment. Many of the tricks are adolescent shenanigans, mostly with sexual overtones, but the description of one is probably the funniest part of the book. Like most WLT performers, Vince Upton reads his scripts for *Story Hour with Grandpa Sam* without going over them before the broadcast. When someone substitutes a raunchy script for the one he should be reading, he does not notice until Cowboy Chuck "pours himself a stiff drink" (6) and launches into a derogatory description of the residents of St. Paul. Vince tries to signal the control room, but no one seems to be there. The description of Pabletta, the love interest, would do justice to the kind of romance called a "bodice ripper." Vince attempts to look ahead, but some of the lines seem innocuous until he has read them aloud. Soon there are "naked bodies slipping around in the sheets moaning and pounding the mattress" (6–7). He tries to make amends by muttering, "Of course, I knew I should not have done this" (7). Although he is panicked by the thought of speaking impromptu, when he gets to Chuck's removing Pabletta's shirt when they are swimming in a lake, Vince can take no more. He throws away the script and ad libs, sending Chuck to a church where he asks his mother for forgiveness. Pabletta gets hit by a truck. Then after telling all his young listeners to obey their parents and go to church, Vince gratefully signs off.

A similar incident occurs years later when Patsy Konopka, who writes the innocuous scripts for most of the shows, livens up one by turning a newly arrived character into an exotic dancer. Patsy later claims that she writes risqué pages to keep herself awake; she just forgot to remove these from the final script. Because the actress playing the dancer is Maria Antonio, of whom Patsy is jealous, the excuse is questionable, but like the earlier broadcast, the results when the script is read on the air produce one of the funnier parts of the novel. This time the actors are less reluctant to extemporize after they realize that the script is inappropriate. Nevertheless, with several people doing the ad libbing and a sound effects person trying to keep up, the results are quite funny. When someone sends the handyman to tend to her clematis, the sound person is bewildered. He has no idea what kind of noise a clematis makes.

Other sexual activity involves not scripts but people. Ray Soderbjerg is a ladies' man who travels to New York twice a year, sometimes with his wife Vesta, but often with another woman. When he travels with Vesta, the trip is "all High Purpose" (33), and they visit museums and other cultural attractions. When he travels with any of the young women, the purpose is very different. Then it is all self-indulgence, from the best hotel and the best food to the best entertainment, which includes the attentions of the young woman. Over the years Ray takes women from all walks of life, but many are his own employees. He even has a bedroom above his office, the purpose of which is obvious. Nevertheless, he has a clear rule for everyone else: *"No Sex On The Premises"* (276). It is this rule that eventually ties in the sexual chapters to the two basic plot lines.

When the Reverend Irving James Knox, who does the station's meditations and vespers, is caught trying to seduce someone from the typing pool, he is chastised by Roy Jr. but not fired. Roy contends that the staff is just following Ray's example, but Ray warns it is a serious mistake not to fire him. Ray appears to be right. An outbreak of office hankypanky occurs, culminating in a liaison between Hazel Park, a valuable office worker, and Wendell Shepherd, a member of the gospel quartet that regularly does *The Rise and Shine Show*. After two weeks Wendell drops Hazel, who is so distraught she has to go home to Mankato for a month. When she does return, she is so changed that her boss finds out the truth about the short-lived affair.

Roy Jr. determines to punish Wendell and in the process to get rid of several others who have not been doing their jobs. The most effective punishment he can contrive is to send them on a three-week tour of Minnesota. Having to do *The Rise and Shine Show* at 6:00 A.M., a second show at noon, and a concert in the evening would be a strenuous enough schedule, but to do those performances while racing from one stop to another on a small bus on which they must sleep will make the tour seem like penance. In addition to the Shepherds, Roy Jr. sends Slim Graves, a "whiny" engineer named Barney, and a drummer. And he sends Frank to take care of them. He explains, "I want them to suffer a little but I don't want them to die in a ditch and I don't want them going through Lyons County raping and pillaging. You're going to see to it. You're going to save them from themselves" (290).

Having just begun his announcing career, Frank is reluctant to go, but Roy Jr. is clear that even though he hopes the performers will get disgusted and quit, he wants Frank to return. The trip is like an undeserved hell for Frank. He is shocked at the behavior of Slim and the Shepherds, who are drunk most of the time on Everclear, the preferred drink of gospel singers because it cannot be detected on the breath. He is also afraid for his life when the bus hurtles through the night at ninety miles an hour on icy roads. Despite playing in high schools to an audience of sixteen, the tour does not hit bottom until they run into a blizzard. They have to change broadcast sites from a church to the only open business in town, a restaurant frequented by "hefty men in flannel shirts glumly chewing" (339). One of the hefty men does not take kindly to having his bacon and eggs interrupted by a broadcast and he picks a fight. The result is a free-for-all from which the radio crew barely escapes. Only when they get to their bus do they realize that the whole altercation has been broadcast and that they are still on the air. Frank has to return to the restaurant, and they listen to his footsteps as he walks across the room to pull the plug on the equipment.

The incident is a pivotal point for all involved. Even though they have a performance scheduled for noon, Elmer, one of the Shepherds, voices the thoughts of the others: "I think this is the Lord's way of telling us to move on" (349). He has a friend who owns a Bible camp not far away where he knows they can stay a few days, and he announces that they are through with WLT. Everyone but Frank is jubilant. They cheer at the thoughts of real beds and warm showers and are buoyed by the prospect of abandoning the tour. Not so, Frank. He muses, *"My job. . . . I can't throw away my job"* (349). Even though the job may have been impossible to complete, he was instructed to get the performers through their tour as well as make them want to quit radio. He has accomplished the latter goal but not the former. As he is pondering what to do, he comes to another terrible realization. The $800 Roy Jr. gave him for emergencies is gone. Someone on the bus has taken it.

By the time the bus pulls into the camp, Frank is in a quandary. He cannot go back to WLT a failure. At least if he can find the money, he can redeem himself in one way. By staying awake later than the rest of his WLT crew, he finds the money hidden carefully in a Bible, and he leaves the camp immediately. He grabs a train for Duluth, planning to return to WLT. Then on the train he begins to wonder whether that is wise. It will take too long to regain Roy Jr.'s trust after abandoning his charges. Besides, he thinks radio is dead; listeners are leaving radio for television. In Duluth he inquires whether a train on the other side of the platform is going to Minneapolis, but when he finds it is going to Chicago, he gets on.

The plot lines separate again as Keillor brings everything to a close. As the $800 on which Frank has lived for three months is about to run out, a lucky bit of timing puts him in a television newscaster's job at WGN. In contrast, everything at WLT seems to be dying including Ray

Soderbjerg, who has cancer. Frank discovers this when he calls Maria and asks her to come to Chicago to marry him. Long-running shows come to an end as the principal actors decide it is time to retire from some and Roy Jr. closes others. As two actors from *Friendly Neighbor* leave the building after the last performance, one notices that the radio shops that used to line the street are all gone. They realize that one can no longer even buy a radio around there. The era of radio has run its course.

WLT: A Radio Romance concludes with an epilogue that takes place forty years later. It concerns an academic who is writing an unauthorized biography of Frank White. Frank has gone on to become famous and thus prey for an unscrupulous writer. The writer fantasizes about incidents that, if they only happened, could make his book a best-seller. He clearly antagonizes some people he interviews by expecting only negative information, but some oblige by telling erroneous stories or distorting what did happen. He even contemplates luring Frank to his death so that he can have a fitting end to the biography. For Keillor this is payback time. Because he was very annoyed at an unauthorized biography written about himself, he gives this writer absurd ideas and shows him to have preconceived notions that he tries to get confirmed by those he interviews.

Keillor may have gotten personal satisfaction from portraying the biographer in this way, but the epilogue is not a particularly effective ending to the novel. The story really ends in the preceding chapter. With that chapter, Keillor has completed the romance of radio. He has presented its infancy, its bloom, and its decline. At one point in the novel Frank concludes that he has "unlocked the secret of radio" (281). It is, as an actor told him, having the "genius to elevate the ordinary," and although Frank considers himself "an ordinary genius" (281), it is radio that excelled at making entertainment from the mundane. By 1951, however, television was already beginning to take over the role of glorifying the pedestrian activities and ideas of ordinary people. Even though radio would later find an alternative role that would keep it alive, the romance was dead.

CHARACTER DEVELOPMENT

Despite the fact that he does not appear until chapter 10, Francis With is the central protagonist of *WLT: A Radio Romance*. The reader first meets him when he writes a letter to Little Becky, a character on WLT's *Friendly Neighbor*. In that series Little Becky's father has left her with the Bensons while he travels with a woman not his wife. Most of the fan letters to Becky are thankful that she is now with people who will care for her. Fans send her food and tell her she is their favorite radio personality. Francis's letter is different in two ways: instead of mailing it, he carries it with him to the station, and instead of talking about Becky, he talks about himself. Francis explains that he lives with his parents, his sister Jodie, and his grandfather in Mindren, North Dakota. He thinks the experiences of his grandfather when he arrived in this country from Denmark would be appropriate stories to tell on the program and offers to send them if Becky is interested.

In addition to giving the reader immediate insight into Francis's preoccupation with self, the letter hints at the entrepreneurial spirit that is another of his characteristics. Already at ten, he is trying to take advantage of every opportunity that comes his way. He knows that possibilities may open up if the stories are told on the air. He works hard at improving himself by improving his vocabulary. In order to learn five new words a day, he writes down all new words he hears, and he belongs to the Word Club of *The Children's Hour* magazine. His conversation when he tries to use the words from the club list is funny. Although he occasionally uses a new word correctly, more often he says such things as "I am very *amenable* to passing you the salt with *alacrity*" (88).

Francis's habit of making lists serves him well when he starts work at WLT. There he makes lists about everything connected with the station— past history, current procedures, actors, owners. This methodical approach to his job, coupled with his dependability, makes him a very useful employee and enables him to move from errand boy to announcer at WLT. The knowledge he gains from observing others is what gives him the ability to succeed at the Chicago television station at the end.

Francis's intensity and determination are admirable characteristics, but he has other traits that are less admirable. He seems emotionally limited. Whether his feelings are stunted by his father's sudden death and his mother's inability to cope with her loss is not clear. If Francis grieves, he internalizes his grief. One can understand the pain caused by callous schoolmates who sing terrible songs about the train wreck, and one can even understand the vulnerability of a child who sings with them just so he can gain friends and be admired, but Francis seems to feel little guilt or faithlessness after that incident. He does write his dead father one of several letters, but he does not seem to be sorry in any way.

Another important character is Ray Soderbjerg. Typical of many ambitious businessmen of the 1920s, Ray becomes successful through a combination of chutzpah and luck. He is forward looking in his ideas and courageous in his decisions. He may complain about business and worry about what could happen, but when pushed to act, he does so boldly. He borrows $20,000 to boost the wattage of the station; he sells the restaurant when it becomes a drag on the broadcasting business; he moves WLT to the Ogden Hotel when it needs more space. All his brave moves pay off and bring growth to the station and wealth to Ray. Leaving the daily administration of the station to his nephew Roy Jr., Ray concentrates on what he does best—the big picture, the big idea.

Ray's commendable attributes of foresight and pluck are somewhat negated by another personal character trait. Ray is a womanizer. Early in the novel he tells his nephew, "I have yet to regret a single moment I spent alone with a beautiful woman" (10), and the book mentions many. Ironically Ray is adamant that the station maintain the highest standards of what could be called family values. Roy Jr. takes him to task for his hypocrisy, pointing out that he chases every woman around. Ray's response is simple: "Every sinner has high ideals" (27). Ray is a crude pragmatist whose temerity one salutes, but whose excesses one deprecates. Only when he is dying does he become a sympathetic character. Then his ability to face imminent death is laudable.

Among the few women whom Ray Soderbjerg is unable to seduce is Patsy Konopka. One of the most complex characters in *WLT: A Radio Romance*, Patsy begins her radio career as an alto in a singing group, the Radio Cowgirls. When Ray notices her and inveigles her into the bedroom above his office, he is the one who is in for a surprise. In response to his line about the look in her eyes, she says it is due to theosophy and positivism. She studies his nimbus and accurately pronounces, "You are swift of intuition, but you lack depth. . . . And you are trying to get me to take my clothes off" (61). As he tries to undress her, she talks of emanations, and when he guesses the wrong color of her nimbus, she rebuffs him. She does, however, mention that she is tired of yodeling and wants to be a writer. Hoping that providing that opportunity will get him in her good graces, Ray hires her to write instead of sing.

Patsy's positivistic ideas, which advocate writing freely without editing, enable her to become the most prolific writer at WLT and to pour out scripts for multiple shows. She is one of the many WLT employees who live at the Antwerp, and when Francis comes to live there, he takes the apartment immediately above Patsy's. In fact, there is an opening in the kitchen that enables Patsy to hear every movement from the apartment above. That situation provides the impetus for a crush that Patsy develops on the younger Frank. She does not even know who he is at the beginning; she just falls for the sounds of the person above her. When she finally discovers his name and something about him, she carries on a fantasy courtship that is rudely spoiled by the advent of Maria.

Patsy's tenure at WLT lasts as long as her relationship with Ray. Even when she gets sloppy and forgets characters or plot lines, no one suggests firing her because of Ray's patronage. Yet Ray is never able to be anything other than a patron to Patsy. When he is dying and his wife Vesta is in London, Patsy nurses him. She even sleeps in the same bed, but that is as close as he gets to realizing his goal. When Ray dies, she takes all the boxes of her scripts, places them in Studio B, and leaves.

In the epilogue Patsy tells the biographer that she hated the years at WLT, but that is a revisionist look from the bitter feminist poet she has become. At the time that she is there, she changes from a young idealist to a recluse almost totally absorbed in her writing and her daydreams. As she gradually becomes more removed from the operations of the station, the reader gets the feeling of separation but not animosity.

THEMATIC ISSUES

A common subject of many American novels is the frontier. Often that frontier is physical. As the geographic frontier in the United States moved constantly westward, the setting of frontier novels moved from the Appalachian Mountains to the Great Plains to the Wild West. A growing nation has other frontiers, however. Some are found in those areas of human endeavor in which enterprising people establish cities, build industries, or make medical breakthroughs. In *WLT: A Radio Romance*, Garrison Keillor depicts life on the frontier of radio. He pays tribute to the medium in all its manifestations while simultaneously exposing its ugliness. Like a Western cow town with saloons, gun slingers, and fancy women in addition to the town stalwarts, his radio has reprobates, lechers, and incompetents with only Vesta trying to use radio for some positive purpose.

No matter how much Keillor personally loves radio, his theme seems to be that the medium has not lived up to its potential. It might have been a vehicle for transmitting the finest of human efforts. It could have been a showcase for creative ventures in all but the visual arts. Had radio scheduled drama, music, and thoughtful discussions about important issues, people in the remotest areas would have had access to a region's foremost talent and best ideas. While radio in its heyday actually did broadcast the New York Philharmonic and the Metropolitan Opera, most programs, like those at WLT, were vacuous shows geared toward entertaining people without making them think. Actors made successful careers by reading inane scripts over the air. They were idolized by fans who fed their fame by worshiping it.

In many a Western a marshall rides into town to set things right and give the residents hope for an orderly existence where human decency will be valued and ideas rather than money will be prized. Early in *WLT* Vesta objects to the addition of commercials because she realizes they are aimed at tying down women, trying to convince them that merit lies in better cooking or housekeeping. She is alarmed that a medium that could have been used for education is being used to sell toilet bowl cleaner. In an echoing of Keillor's theme, she tells Ray, "This could have been the Acropolis . . . and you made it a bazaar" (152).

ALTERNATE READING: DECONSTRUCTION

A popular form of criticism in the twentieth century is deconstruction, but to understand the development of deconstruction, one must go back to a preceding kind of criticism called structuralism. Structuralism is based on the theories of a Swiss linguist named Ferdinand de Saussure. Saussure argues that a word is not a representation of something to which it refers, as linguists before him maintained. Instead he calls words signs and divides them into two parts: the signifier and the signified. The spoken or written word is the signifier; it is what one hears or reads. The signified is the concept for which the signifier stands (Bressler 92). "Probably Saussure's most important argument [is] that no intrinsic relationship obtains between the two parts of the sign, the signifier and the signified" (Atkins 16). Instead of having a natural link, the signifier and the signified combine to form the sign. "The person seeing the word *tree* has in mind both the sound and the concept" (Stevens and Stewart 34).

The person most closely associated with deconstruction, Jacques Derrida, borrows from Saussure the idea that "meaning in language is determined by the differences among the language signs" (Bressler 123). Derrida concludes that Western metaphysics is founded on a set of binary oppositions, one of which is valued over the other. In other words, for every center of unity, there is a decentered center of unity. One understands light because of dark, silence because of noise. Among the steps suggested by Charles Bressler as a means of deconstructing a text are recognizing the binary oppositions, reversing them, and exploring new meanings based on the reversals (131). Placing more value on one opposition in a pair is invalid. Joseph Culler explains that an aim of deconstruction is "to show how [a discourse] undermines the philosophy it asserts, or the hierarchical oppositions on which it relies" (86).

One can find oppositions in *WLT: A Radio Romance* with regard to good and evil. This is particularly evident in the differences between the values projected by various radio shows and those exhibited by the people who create them. In a review Anne Bernays says of Keillor's characters: "Nearly all the people in this book have something wrong with them— they are liars, hypocrites, self-deceivers, sex addicts, sad grotesques or egomaniacs." The minister who gives sermonettes for the station preys on young women. The flashily dressed members of a gospel quartet are guilty of more than bad taste. Although they sing about Christian virtues, they live degenerate lives, spending most of their time drinking, carousing, and womanizing. Even Lily Dale, really Roy and Ray Soderbjerg's sister Lottie, is not the young and beautiful singer her fans think her to be but an aging, grotesquely fat drug addict.

The sharpest oppositions can be seen on the long-running show *Friendly Neighbor*. The show centers around Dad Benson, owner of a feed store in the small town of Elmville. Dad lives with his daughter Jo and her husband Frank. Dad is a generous man whose thoughtfulness and sensitivity endear him to women in the radio audience. Women in the scripts also find him attractive, but he is faithful to his wife, who lies comatose in a nursing home. Little Becky joins this family group when her father deposits her there so he can have a more private visit with his paramour Ginger. In actual fact, almost all the characters are distinct contrasts to the actors who play them. Marjery Moore, the teenager who portrays the innocent Little Becky, is so crude in both speech and actions that she fails to amuse even the most jaded of her companions. Every listener to the show contrasts the philandering of Becky's father with the fidelity of Dad Benson, but the real Dad Benson has a ten-year affair with Faith Snelling, who plays Jo, his radio daughter.

There are also oppositions on a more specific level. One involves Maria Antonio. When Frank is sent on tour with the Shepherd Boys, he is reluctant to leave Maria, whom he has been dating. He proposes to her, hoping she will come along on the tour. Maria, however, is unclear how she feels about Frank. She still has regard for Merle, who befriended her during acting school days. She admits confusion and refuses to consider the proposal. While Frank is gone, Merle visits her, and she goes to bed with him. The act, which could be construed as a betrayal of Frank, actually works to his advantage. While Maria is still in bed with Merle, she realizes that she loves Frank. By learning that she does not want Merle, she understands what she does want.

It is human nature to suspect goodness. Often readers find the good boring. They long for something a bit more exciting, more titillating. However, in *WLT: A Radio Romance* Keillor does not confine himself to presenting repugnant characters who engage in reprehensible acts. Through the gossip and the exaggerated tales his characters tell, Keillor manages to get in dirty songs, dirty jokes, and dirty pranks. The book is so filled with flatulence and fornication that the reader longs for someone to exhibit self-control, to do what is right, to be—good. In opposition to what he seems to be glorifying, Keillor creates a desire for goodness.

8

The Book of Guys
(1993)

In *The Book of Guys*, Garrison Keillor returned to writing short fiction. The book's dust jacket bears a copy of *Four Officers of the Amsterdam Coopers and Wine Rackers*, a painting by Gerbrand van den Eeckhout on which Keillor's picture is superimposed. The people in Keillor's stories are not figures from 1657 trade guilds, however, but a mix of mythological figures from ancient Greece, characters from Mozart operas, and contemporary people from the United States. What the stories have in common is their theme, the male experience.

As with two earlier collections of pieces unrelated to Lake Wobegon, this group contains several stories that first appeared in the *New Yorker*. One story, "That Old Picayune-Moon," appeared first in *Harper's*, and "George Bush" was previously collected in *We Are Still Married* under the title "How the Savings and Loans Were Saved."

The introduction, which Keillor presents as a speech to the National Federation of Associations, sets up the theme of the book. Supposedly Keillor's first-person narrator won a membership in the Sons of Bernie, a group dedicated to drinking and male bonding in a backwoods setting. The speaker claims to be repelled by the "low-lifes" with whom he is associating until he drinks enough to begin feeling brotherly. After songs and jokes, the men begin to talk about women. The speaker admits he feels excited as he realizes they are saying things they would not normally say in polite society, which he translates as meaning in front of females. One man complains that he discovered his wife actually enjoyed being pregnant; another grumbles about affirmative action; still another tells the tale of Bernie, a man whose wife became a feminist.

The speaker realizes that "guys are in trouble" (10). Back in the male heyday, he explains, women died for men. He gives examples from opera and Shakespeare: "Carmen *stabbed to death*, Butterfly *self-stabbed*, Tosca *self-hurled from parapet*, Brunhilde *self-burned*, Aïda *self-buried*, Ophelia *swam after mealtime*" (11–12). Today women evaluate men to see whether they measure up to current standards of acceptability. After recounting the accomplishments of everyone from Plato to Van Gogh, he laments that once "manhood was an opportunity for achievement, and now it is a problem to be overcome" (11).

Stories in *The Book of Guys* dramatize the situations in which men find themselves. Some are specific like that of Buddy the Leper, but others are universal like the midlife crisis suffered by the god of wine. Although the Promise Keepers, a group that holds large male gatherings in sports stadia, was just getting started when this book was written, other male support groups were already well established. Many organizations sponsored events similar to the Guy Pride luncheon attended by Keillor's speaker. Their aim was to help men through their changing societal roles. Still other groups were openly antifeminist. Keillor uses this backdrop for a humorous handling of real problems.

PLOT DEVELOPMENT

The first story in the collection is "Lonesome Shorty," the tale of a cowboy who tries to settle down. Anyone who has heard the "Lives of the Cowboys" segments on *A Prairie Home Companion* will see similarities between those skits and this story. Shorty has had all he can take of the back ends of cows and a horse that steps on him. He analyzes the words of the song "Home on the Range" and comes to the conclusion that they are completely unrealistic. He tells one of his uncommunicative partners, "I'm sorry if this sounds like a discouraging word, but animals do not make for a home" (24).

In contemplation of leaving the range, Shorty makes a list of the good and bad points of a cowboy's life. A cowboy certainly has freedom, but freedom is accompanied by loneliness. He can enjoy beautiful scenery, but unfortunately he has to sleep in it. Instead of standing up for justice on the range, he needs to be building up equity in a home. When he gets the opportunity to become deputy sheriff in the town of Pleasant Gulch, he takes it. He buys a condo and is able to move in immediately, thanks to the shooting death of the former owner. He even buys himself a set of Amaryllis china. His newly acquired domestic comfort is short-lived, however, for stray bullets from a gunfight break some of the china, and his neighbors object to the noise he makes gargling and yodeling. Shorty gets so mad that he packs his china, saddles his horse, and leaves town.

Shorty has an internal conflict that he never resolves. Like many another infected with wanderlust, he is never satisfied with his current situation. On the range he longs for comfort and social interaction, but once in town he is inevitably disappointed, and he retreats once more to life under the open sky. He continues that pattern throughout his life and beyond.

In "The Chuck Show of Television" Keillor satirizes the talk shows of the nineties. Pitted against competition that features guests with various kinds of aberrant behavior, *The Chuck Show* is not doing well in the ratings. As informative as are Chuck's discussions with parents about Minneapolis school buses and vocational counseling, they cannot hold their own against hosts who shred their clothing or people who discuss smelly relatives and myopic berserkers.

A new producer from Chicago, brought in to increase the number of viewers, screams at the staff, insisting that the program quit acting like a civics class. Staff members point out that the Twin Cities area is not known for large numbers of socially challenged people except for alcoholics, whose poor memories make them poor guests. Nevertheless, the program finally makes it to the top of the ratings by turning to animals and showing rabbit sex and chicken hypnosis. Alas, success only brings more problems. *The Chuck Show* must now hunt for excesses in the animal world that will be more shocking than comparable excesses among people.

Conflict between rival shows produces no new heights of instruction or entertainment for viewers. Instead attempts to outdo one another plumb the depths of tasteless diversion. "The Chuck Show of Television" demonstrates the real situation about which Oprah Winfrey spoke in a February 1999 interview. She called daytime television, particularly the show of her rival Jerry Springer, a "vulgarity circus" and vowed to quit daytime television at the end of her contract ("Winfrey").

In Greek myth Theseus is renowned as the Athenian hero who slew the Minotaur and then escaped from the labyrinth with the help of Ariadne, daughter of the king of Crete. Having betrayed her father for love, Ariadne left Crete with Theseus, but she never arrived in Athens. Although stories differ about whether Theseus deliberately abandoned her, they agree that she was left behind on the windy island of Naxos. In one version of the myth, she was rescued by Dionysus, the god of wine and revelry. This is the version on which Keillor bases his story, "The Midlife Crisis of Dionysus."

By the time of the story, Ariadne and Dionysus have been married for years. As the title implies, Dionysus has a problem. He has suddenly had immortality taken from him, and the result is that he must experience the aging process like all humankind. He discovers this abruptly when Gladys, the muse of maturity, arrives in her sensible shoes and announces that he is fifty years old. Then, after he forgoes an orgy to stay at home and work a crossword, Ariadne tells him, "Dio, we need to talk about your drinking" (62). Although he emphasizes that he is not the god of iced tea, she insists that he get help. His attempt to visit his father Zeus on Mount Olympus is delayed when he is bumped from a flight because his deity card has expired. The rest of the tale continues Dionysus's attempts to cope with the unanticipated changes in his life.

The fourth story, "Buddy the Leper," has an improbable subject. Throughout history, leprosy has been one of the most dreaded diseases. Unlike the plague, which usually killed most of its victims, leprosy caused death in life, an existence so horrifying to ancient people that lepers were made to shout "Unclean" as they approached to make sure the unafflicted had time to get far away. Leper colonies were set apart on islands, in valleys, anywhere the victims could be isolated and kept from inadvertently infecting the healthy.

Leprosy, or Hansen's disease, affects both the skin and the nervous system. The skin becomes thickened and discolored while nerve damage leaves the victim subject to unnoticed injuries, paralysis, and deformities of the hands and feet. Today the disease is treatable, but its legacy remains. People still use the term "leper" to mean someone ostracized by society.

There is a shock factor in Keillor's choice of a leper as the protagonist of a story. Readers may laugh, but their laughter comes from discomfort. Yet uncomfortable laughter is often a Keillor aim as is laughter at mixtures of the familiar and the unexpected. There are many such incongruous combinations here. Buddy's father, a Methodist missionary, chooses to live in the African bush rather than in an urban area because he wants Buddy to have "the benefit of a small-town upbringing" (74).

Buddy's mother takes him not to a witch doctor, but to a witch dentist. The father is both a missionary and a saxophonist whose jazz group performs at the Ramada Masada. Masada, the name of an ancient fortress in Israel, conjures up images of a foreign world totally negated by Ramada, a chain of American motels. Finally, Buddy catches the dread disease from a toilet seat. Of all the reasons children have been warned not to sit on public toilet seats, fear of leprosy was not one.

Although Buddy is shunned by everyone in his African village, one might expect his situation to improve when his father is reassigned to South Dakota. People there know nothing of his disease. Their ignorance does not last long, however. At his father's suggestion, he tells people at a Bible camp that he has leprosy and that he regards it as "an opportunity for grace" (78). It is unclear how much grace Buddy earns from that confession, but it totally eliminates any opportunity for him to have friends until Lulu comes to work in the family home. Lulu's name fits her character. She wears a dress that explodes when she wants to take it off in a hurry, and for Buddy she does just that. He observes that "South Dakota is not a touchy place even under the best of circumstances" (84), and Buddy's circumstances have not been good. However, Lulu knows nothing of his leprosy and quickly makes up for all the touching Buddy has missed. She also gives him the confidence to strike out on his own and make a new life for himself among others who are unaware of his disease.

"Mr. St. Paul" is a poem about a body builder. When he is crowned and given the title of Mr. St. Paul, he crows that life could not be better than it is, yet the longer he talks, the more he reveals of an obsession with a lost girlfriend and her present lover. There is no humor in this poem. Instead Keillor gives a glimpse into the mind of those who stalk and sometimes kill. The contrasts between the confidence of the speaker as champion and his fixation as jilted lover, between the perfection of the body and the imperfection of the soul are stark, and the poem ends darkly.

Most letters to the editor are meant for publication, but "That Old Picayune Moon" takes the form of a letter meant for the eyes of the editor only. The letter, written by the mayor of a small town, is a rather adolescent protest against the editor and the paper he runs. What the editor has done is have a photographer follow the mayor and take his picture at uncomfortable moments—when he is adjusting his underwear or rubbing his eyes. That annoys him far more than all the headlines complaining that he, as a four-term mayor, is feeding "at the public trough" (107).

The harassment continues until the photographer gets the picture he wants—of the mayor raving.

Just as he is about to attack the editor in a restaurant, the mayor has a vision of what the paper will become should the editor be incapacitated. The managing editor Delores Whinny will take over, making the paper all sweetness and light. Columnists will write about children, and the sports section will be renamed "Games & Growth." Suddenly the prospect of continued tabloid-style headlines aimed at him seems preferable, particularly since the picture of him raging has aroused his wife.

Danny's problem, so his wife tells him, is that his "life is in Park and the key isn't even in the ignition" (112). "Marooned" is the story of Danny's rivalry with this brother-in-law Dave. When they were young, Danny was the one on the career fast track while Dave gave up working in his father's stationery store to join a commune. However, twenty-five years later, Dave, having inherited the store, has turned it into a successful chain, and Danny has just lost his job. Danny remarks, "I brought lucidity to capitalism, and Dave brought gibberish, and he walked off with the prize" (117).

In the throes of despondency, with his marriage threatened, Danny accepts Dave's offer of $15,000 to take his wife on a two-week private cruise. Danny has a premonition of disaster when the captain mentions that their bedroom is downstairs instead of below decks, but Julie wants to talk about their marriage, not the boat. The title gives away part of what happens but certainly not all.

In "Don Giovanni" Keillor spoofs several operas. He takes Giovanni, the title character of one of Wolfgang Amadeus Mozart's tragic operas, and puts the licentious nobleman into a reworking of *The Marriage of Figaro*, one of Mozart's comic operas. References to the don's attempts to seduce Figaro's wife Susanna on her wedding night smack of Count Almaviva's tries in the latter opera while the incidents with Zerlina are based on *Don Giovanni*.

At the beginning of Keillor's version the don has been reduced to playing piano at a bar in Fargo, North Dakota. He wears flamboyant clothing designed to outdo Liberace, the television pianist popular in the fifties, and gives advice as though he were still the delight of all women in Seville, but this is a worn don, whose arguments are as tawdry as his clothes. Nevertheless, before the story ends there is an interesting counterpoint between Figaro, the marriage supporter, and Don Giovanni, the marriage disparager.

Keillor's love of radio has spawned several short stories as well as

WLT: A Radio Romance. In "Roy Bradley, Boy Broadcaster," he again uses the medium as a backdrop. This time the setting is Piscacatawamaquod-dymoggin, Maine, not Minnesota, but Roy's fascination with radio is similar to that of Francis With in *WLT*. Unlike Francis, however, Roy comes along at the end of radio's heyday. By the time he graduates from high school and is ready to go to broadcasting school or, given his natural talent, directly attempt an announcer's job, television has reduced the opportunities in radio to a very few. In addition to battling the job situation, Roy must battle his own lethargy. The story is resolved when, like radio, he finally finds his niche.

There is no question about the inspiration for "Gary Keillor." In this story Keillor looks back at his own youth, but in capturing the pain and eventual triumph of an insecure adolescent, he tells the story of all young people who have ever felt excluded. While the discovery of what it feels like to work an audience is autobiographical, the sense of achievement when the outsider bests the "in" crowd is universal.

"Omoo the Wolf Boy" bears no resemblance to *Omoo*, the Herman Melville novel set in the South Seas. If anything, this is a reverse of the Roman tale of Romulus and Remus, twins who were raised by a she-wolf, or of Kipling's story of Mowgli in *The Jungle Book*. Instead of being raised by animals and eventually joining people, Omoo does not leave civilization until age eight, when his beloved mother dies and his father remarries. He joins a wolf pack and eventually takes the name of the grandfather wolf. The wolves teach him wolf language while he teaches them Broadway show tunes. Keillor has great fun with this bit of fantasy, particularly with the parts about language. Omoo explains that tense in wolf language is indicated by the angle of one's tail, a requirement that puts him at a distinct disadvantage.

When Omoo is eighteen, one of his wolf brothers takes him aside and tells him he needs to face the fact that he is different: he is not a good hunter, and he speaks with a decided accent. In fact, the brother warns him, "Nobody's going to invite you on the hunt, nobody's going to share his kill with you" (198). He will become the ultimate outcast, a lone wolf. Omoo admits that he is "smell-impaired" but maintains that wolves who cannot hunt should have the same rights as those who can. The wolf pack has never heard of equal opportunity, however, and Omoo finds it expeditious to leave. His reintroduction to the world of humans provides Keillor more opportunity for amusement.

After two short pieces in which Keillor reworks an Aesop fable and a popular poem, he includes another short story. Entitled "Herb Johnson, the God of Canton," it tells of a high school football star whose touch-down runs make him an object of worship. When he goes to college at Indiana State, he continues to elude linebackers. Then in his junior year he tears ligaments in one knee. He sits out several games until Myra Jordan, his coach, asks him to go in for one last play. Her promises induce him to score the tying touchdown despite ruining his knee and ending his football career. There could be great conflict in this story but, as Herb tells it, he never thinks twice about sacrificing all for Myra. He also seems to have no regrets about the way his life has turned out afterwards, or so he says, and says, and says . . . to the point that the reader begins to doubt.

Earl Grey is a tea flavored with oil of bergamot. According to legend, Charles Earl Grey, a British prime minister during the nineteenth cen-tury, originally received this tea as a gift from an envoy to China. It was he who popularized it by serving it to guests in his home. Garrison Keillor does not feel confined by legends, however. In "Earl Grey" he writes his own, attributing the origin of the tea to an American. The challenge for Earl is not to establish a distinguished tea, but to be rec-ognized. Unfortunately, Earl is a middle child, and his middleness seems to affect everything he does. Despite all his accomplishments, his battle to become visible is never won.

Although nothing seems to go right for Earl, nothing seems to go wrong for the titular hero of "Winthrop Thorpe Tortuga." At least that is the way it appears at the beginning. Not only is Winthrop a perfect husband and father, but he is an astute businessman. In three years, one investment pays off at over 28,000 percent. His financial bonanza enables him to stay at home and finish all the projects most men plan but never begin. To make his life complete, he is an avid fan of the Minnesota Twins at a time when they are winning. It seems that Winthrop has and is everything he could wish . . . until he reveals more about himself. This is less a story than a probing character analysis.

"Al Denny" satirizes several phenomena of the latter part of the twen-tieth century. Denny has become successful by combining New Age phi-losophy with the marketing techniques of the PTL Club. As his books, such as *Rebirthing the Me You Used to Be*, sell more and more copies, his autographing sessions and lecture tours bring in millions. Soon his agent Larry sets up a village in Iowa similar to Jim Bakker's Heritage USA in South Carolina. Al is so busy emptying his "being of all havingness" (262) that he is not aware of Larry's activities, which include bilking followers out of their life savings in scams similar to Bakker's selling of bricks and streets. The denouement follows that of the real Bakker story with the FBI knock at the door, but because Al has been taken in by his own New Age silliness, the story's ending is much happier than Bakker's.

After "George Bush," collected in a previous book under a different title, comes "Christmas in Vermont." It is difficult to say what is responsible for the association between that holiday and that state, but for millions of Americans the idea of Christmas in Vermont stirs feelings of nostalgia. Even those who have never set foot in New England feel warm at the thought. Here again Keillor combines targets for his satire. One is the traditional. The wealthy family in the story decorates for the season with "traditional" items even though the traditions can be from diverse cultures. Thus they have "traditional" Navaho streamers and "traditional" French-Canadian wreaths over a "traditional" Shaker fireplace. For all, they have paid much more than traditional prices. Interspersed throughout the story are come-ons from the author for artistic support. They include opportunities for readers to buy such items as sweaters made by "authentic elderly rural women" (295).

The author claims that he started writing with a grant from Bert and Willy's Ice Cream. That gives Keillor a chance to tweak Ben and Jerry, the ice cream entrepreneurs who really were flower children and who have maintained their social conscience by controlling the wage disparity between labor and management and by including environmental messages on their packaging. The laughs at the expense of Ben and Jerry are good-natured, much more than those aimed at all who prefer a sentimentalized ideal instead of the real.

"Norman Conquest" has a title more appealing than the story. Norman is a writer who specialized in writing crude joke books. His wife, a bovine periodontist, became so exasperated with his snot and fart humor that she told him she wished he would write a novel. Then she was killed in an automobile crash. When the story opens, Norman is trying to write a novel as a kind of tribute to his wife. His joke books may have relied on an audience with a sixth-grade sense of humor, but his novel will have difficulty finding an audience at all. The plot centers on an agoraphobic man who has a relationship with Fred, his refrigerator.

Keillor ends the book with the best story in the collection. It is "Zeus the Lutheran." Zeus, the supreme male god in Greek mythology, is a known philanderer who has a penchant for mortal women. In order to bed them, he frequently takes another form. He reaches the imprisoned Danaë by turning himself into a golden shower; he lures Europa as a comely bull; to catch Leda off guard, he transforms himself into a swan. His repeated affairs make his wife Hera so miserable that she becomes a suspicious nag.

In Keillor's version of the story, Hera sends a lawyer to confront Zeus as he sits in a cafe on the island of Patmos. Zeus is not alarmed. He simply turns the lawyer into salad dressing, pours him over his spinach salad, and tells the waiter to feed the salad to the pigs. Then he orders a young woman. His usual way of handling opposition, "senseless violence followed by easy sex" (319) does not seem to give satisfaction this time, however. He is already bored with the young woman when a cruise ship pulls in. There standing on deck are Wes and his wife Diane. Wes is a Lutheran minister who has been given a two-week trip by his congregation in Pennsylvania. What could have been a second honeymoon has not turned out that way. Rather, Wes and Diane have argued so much that Diane has asked for a separation.

Zeus spots Diane just as Wes is pleading with her. When he raises his arms, Zeus possesses Wes's body, and to complete the metamorphosis, Wes enters an old dog on the dock. From that point on, the challenge for Zeus is to make love to this beautiful woman when confined by "dismal Lutheran thoughts" (326).

CHARACTER DEVELOPMENT

The Book of Guys contains more real short stories than do Keillor's other collections. Consequently, there are also more well-developed characters. One in particular is the protagonist in "Buddy the Leper." Because he is a missionary's child, Buddy is expected to be a model to others. Unlike the traditional "preacher's kid," who rebels against being held to such high standards, Buddy does meet parental expectations, but he does so to his own detriment. He gets leprosy because his mother insists he set an example and use a toilet instead of the bushes. After the family returns to the States, he is unable to make friends because his father urges him to testify about his disease. As a result, he is as shunned and vilified in South Dakota as he was in Africa.

In trying to come to terms with his situation, Buddy reveals acute self-knowledge. He knows that some people have used persecution as a spur to their genius, but he admits that in the heavens of life he is not a star but merely "a small dim moon" (80). When reporters advise him to shoot people rather than repress anger and ruin his life, Buddy tells them that, as the son of missionaries, he would find that difficult to do. He is also practical; he thinks it would be hard to find a gun. Nevertheless, he is intrigued by the idea. Every time fellow students look at him with disgust, he imagines what it would be like to blow them away. He finds it "nice to have homicide as a possibility" (82).

At one time that idea would have been humorous because of its absurdity. For untroubled people, homicide is never a possibility. However, this story was written before the recent spate of high school killings. In light of those atrocities, today's reader knows it would not be difficult for Buddy to find a gun, nor would using homicide to avenge slights, real or imagined, be absurd. It has happened far too often.

Thankfully, Buddy uses violence only in his imagination. As soon as Lulu comes to work for the family, he realizes that he has finally met someone who does not know about his disease, and he concentrates on developing a relationship with her. Although that relationship may also be deemed inappropriate for a missionary child, it is positive in the sense that it gives him the confidence he needs to strike out on his own.

Buddy has tried to obey the commandment to honor his father and mother, but that commandment presupposes parents who are worthy of honor, and Buddy's self-absorbed father and alcoholic mother are not. Only when Buddy sees that he also has a duty to honor himself is he able to move on to what the reader hopes will be a productive, if independent, life.

One of the most intriguing characters in *The Book of Guys* is Winthrop Thorpe Tortuga in the story of the same name. In the first two paragraphs Winthrop seems overwhelmed by good fortune, for which he is smugly grateful. The only hint that he may not deserve such bliss is his use of an ethnic epithet. However, by the third paragraph, the picture of a perfect life starts to come apart. Winthrop may be a dutiful father who attends church and fixes Sunday omelettes for his family, but he also allows teenagers to get drunk at the sixteenth birthday party of his younger daughter; he lets her sleep with her boyfriend in her upstairs bedroom.

The reader gradually realizes that the Tortuga family is completely dysfunctional. Winthrop's older daughter and son are alienated from both the family and society, and his wife is having an affair with her chiropractor. Rather than objecting to any of their activities, Winthrop congratulates himself on his understanding. He seems unaware that his support makes him what contemporary psychologists call a codependent, one who enables the person with a problem to continue his or her unhealthy activity rather than seek help. He allows his son to curse him, he sends money to his unemployed older daughter, and he fixes breakfast for his wife when she returns from a night with her lover.

In his relationships with all of the members of his family, Winthrop carries the principles of tolerance to an irrational extreme, but such patience comes at a cost. He takes out his frustration in a variety of acts, each more despicable than the other. Not content with writing hate letters and calling in bomb threats, he resorts to such acts as honking at the elderly when they are slow in crossing streets and pushing revolving doors when handicapped people are inside.

Winthrop is worse than a hypocrite because, in addition to deluding others, he deludes himself. His lack of awareness of the activities of his family indicates a lack of concern for which his cleaning the garage and paneling the basement do not atone. Winthrop Thorpe Tortuga may be proud of himself, but the reader pities him.

THEMATIC ISSUES

Not only does *The Book of Guys* contain more real stories than the other Keillor collections of short works, but more of the pieces were written specifically for the book rather than for publication elsewhere. Consequently, Keillor has been able to develop in many of the stories variations of the same theme. That theme is the one alluded to in the introduction: the attempts of men to come to terms with their condition, particularly their relationships with women.

One aspect of that relationship is male-female communication. In criticizing marriage, Don Giovanni characterizes the typical wife as one who asks, "Why don't we ever talk to each other?" (135). He complains that a woman asking that question does not wish to talk at all but is instead picking a fight in which she is striking the first blow. Other protagonists are not as recalcitrant as the don, but they are still skeptical. Although Lonesome Shorty is tempted to marry Leonora, he balks because of communication problems. She asks what is he thinking. When he replies that he is thinking of nothing, she responds, "Silence is a form of anger" (33). In "Marooned," at a time when Danny is concerned that their boat and its captain are having difficulty, his wife asks him why they cannot converse in an amicable fashion instead of arguing. These situations provide humor, but they also express the male idea that women tend to talk things, particularly relationships, to death.

Don Giovanni proclaims, "Marriage is for women" (133). Although

Keillor does not necessarily agree, he explains in the introduction that women are better prepared for adult life, a part of which is usually marriage. He bases his argument on the fact that small boys are often sent outside to play while girls are allowed to stay in the house and practice role-playing with dolls. When boys become men and try to be good fathers and monogamous husbands, they are just behaving like trained bears. They can keep pedaling the bicycles they have been taught to ride, but they would really rather be out in the forest.

That seems to be the situation of Figaro. When the don asserts that women, after years of oppression, can now get away with anything and blame it on menopause or premenstrual syndrome while "a married guy is responsible for everything" (134), Figaro does not agree. He maintains that he would be miserable without marriage and Susanna. Nevertheless, he keeps the don's discarded silver jacket and retrieves it every time Susanna throws it out. It seems to symbolize his bit of forest.

According to Keillor, girls know everything about guys, and guys "know nothing about girls except that they want one desperately" (13). He asks, "Which gender is better equipped to manipulate the other?" (13). The story with the most manipulation is "Herb Johnson, God of Canton." In it Herb sacrifices his college athletic career and his future all to please Myra. Few of the other male protagonists go that far, but several do have little control over the situations in which they find themselves. They have come up against strong women and have either deferred to them or moved on.

A few of the pieces in this collection criticize the tactics of the media or poke fun at popular psychology and the pretensions of its followers, but most stick to the main theme. Keillor seems to be saying, "This is the male predicament. Please be gentle."

ALTERNATE READING: READER-RESPONSE CRITICISM

People respond to the arts. When they hear a Mahler symphony, contemplate a Raphael painting, or watch a Tchaikovsky ballet, they are emotionally moved. When they read a novel or see a play, they react. Reader-response criticism concentrates on that reaction. Unlike New Criticism, which focuses on the literary work itself, Reader-response focuses on the reader. The fact that all readers do not have the same response is considered an asset of this kind of criticism (Lynn 7).

In the *Poetics* Aristotle writes, "Tragedy, then, is an imitation of an action of high importance, . . . by means of pity and fear effecting its purgation of these emotions" (24). Clearly the concern for audience re-action goes back as far as Aristotle, but as a form of criticism, Reader-response is fairly new. It had its genesis in the 1930s with the theories of Louise M. Rosenblatt and finally flowered in the 1970s.

Rosenblatt's *Literature as Exploration* was written to help teachers in-terest their students in literature. In it she held that the reader's role is active rather than passive. As a consequence, she admonished, "The greater the reader's ability to respond fully to the stimulus of the word, and the greater his capacity to savor all that the writer can accomplish, the more fully will he be able emotionally and intellectually to participate in the literary work as a whole" (59). From those seminal ideas, Rosen-blatt developed her theory that reading becomes a transaction between a reader and the work of literature being read. It naturally follows that readers with wide reading experience and long life experience will not have the same response as young readers who have read little. One need not agree with Norman Holland, one of Rosenblatt's successors, that all interpretations of literature are valid in order to understand that they will all be subjective. For that reason, Reader-response is of necessity less formal than other forms of criticism. It often uses first person, and it draws on personal experience outside the ken of other readers. A Reader-response reading might go something like this:

In "Gary Keillor," one of the stories in *The Book of Guys*, Garrison Keillor accurately captures the range of emotions that accompany the teen years. I know that the first-person narrator is a created speaker, not the author, but Keillor would not have chosen that particular title had none of the story been true. Perhaps the specific events are all created, but I can't help believing that as a teenager himself Keillor experienced some of the same feelings as those expressed by Gary.

I'm sure I'm not the only person who remembers what it was like to grow too fast or too slow, to stick out when all I wanted to do was blend in. There are a few people who always seem to be the right size, have the right clothes, share the right interests, but most teenagers go through agony until they mature enough to accept themselves as they are. Gary is the typical teen outsider. He loves from afar, the object of his affection being Dede, the chair of the school talent show. When she scorns his offer to participate, he is hurt, but his reaction is not to wilt and go away. Instead her derision makes him determined to enter after all. His resolve is reinforced when he sees his mother stand up to a truck driver who has ruined her flower bed. If his mother, the mildest of women, can find the backbone to face down the opposition, so can he. He gets his opportunity when his English teacher, who happens to be the talent show sponsor, asks him to recite "O Captain! My Captain!" Walt Whitman would not recognize it as Gary presents it, but performing gives Gary a chance for comeuppance.

I don't know what it is about human nature that makes us love an underdog, but we respond more favorably to the runner who comes from behind than to the one who leads from the start. We love it when a person can use a special skill to triumph over the favorite, and we find that triumph even more satisfying if the favorite is smug and the underdog is sympathetic. In "Gary Keillor" the favorite is Bill Swenson, Dede's boyfriend. He thinks himself Mr. Cool, but he lacks the essential characteristic of a performer: good timing. Although Bill's lip-synch of an Elvis tune is the expected success, he doesn't have the sense to leave his audience begging for more, and he does a disastrous encore. Gary, however, not only has good timing, but he can improvise. The result is a triumph for Gary and for the reader because the underdog has come through.

Whether or not Keillor is writing about feelings he actually experienced as a teenager, he is writing about feelings most teenagers have. What he gives us all is not just a sense of identification but a sense of encouragement. If Gary Keillor can come out on top, perhaps there is hope for us all.

9

Wobegon Boy
(1997)

As a youth, Garrison Keillor dreamed of writing for the *New Yorker*, but he found fame by telling radio audiences about the fictional Lake Wobegon and its inhabitants. His dual yearnings for the sophistication of New York and the innocence of "the town that time forgot" create a division in his written work. He alternates between the material aimed at Lake Wobegon aficionados and the pieces that appeal to more urbane readers. After two collections and a novel of the latter type, in *Wobegon Boy* Keillor returns to the lake.

Wobegon Boy tells the story of Johnny Tollefson, whom readers have already met in two sections of *Lake Wobegon Days*. In that earlier book, Johnny is introduced in the section called "Summer." He goes to register for college and is chagrined at being accompanied by beaming relatives eager to share his special day. In "Revival," the last section of the book, he has completed his freshman year and returned to Lake Wobegon, where he is as uncomfortable with his parents as they are with him. *Wobegon Boy* is the story of the same character minus the teenage angst.

According to an old saw, "You can take the boy out of the country, but you can't take the country out of the boy." Although *Wobegon Boy* is the story of John Tollefson's life after leaving Lake Wobegon, it is clear that in many ways John has never left at all. The older he gets, the closer he gets to his birthplace, his birthright, his home.

PLOT DEVELOPMENT

In a first person narration John Tollefson tells his story. If anything, his life is too comfortable once he leaves home. He seems to have no challenge, no purpose. He looks back on his thirties and realizes that his life has been easy but shallow. Thus he introduces both the internal conflict of the novel and its theme: the search for purpose in life.

John recounts that at ten he began reading the Flambeau Family mystery novels, becoming so engrossed in them that he reshelved them under Foreign Language so that no one else could find them and check them out of the library. The Flambeaus, who resided in a New York apartment overlooking Central Park, became his "secret family" (5). The family consisted of Emile, a microbiologist, his actress wife Eileen, and their son Tony, a teenager who attended a private school and excelled in both athletics and schoolwork. Despite their busy professional and academic lives, the Flambeaus somehow managed to find time for both crime solving and socializing. Their forays to museums, elegant restaurants, and the opera made a lasting impression on John. "For a boy whose dad ran the grain elevator in a small town where nobody had ever seen a ballet or knew a gimlet from a grommet, the Flambeaus were an inspiration" (5).

Like Keillor himself, John grew up with dreams of living in New York, but he does not actually leave Minnesota until he is thirty. Then, rather than hurrying toward New York, he is hurrying away from Minneapolis. The immediate reason is to get out of marrying a girl he does not love. John and Korlyss find themselves in one of those situations into which people sometimes drift. Having met at the university, they stay together for ten years out of habit. Only when Korlyss begins to pressure John to marry her does he get the nerve to leave.

He applies for the job of general manager of a new public radio station on the campus of a small but heavily endowed Episcopal college in Red Cliff, New York. On the basis of one legitimate recommendation and another that he wrote himself, he gets the job. Soon he finds himself on the neatly manicured campus of St. James College, where "financially gifted parents" send "academically challenged students" (7), correctly supposing that large enough expenditures will guarantee a diploma. While giving John a tour of the campus, and the deserted library in particular, the dean comments that what the college needs is not a radio station but a literacy program. Nevertheless, John is charmed by the town, the fact that houses are appreciated for their age, that people do not replace everything that begins to look old as they do in Minnesota. He takes the job, believing that he has found a home.

At first things go very well for John. He hires staff members, and by Labor Day of 1985, WSJO goes on the air. He buys a comfortable home at a cheap price and furnishes it with antiques from an auction barn. Thus he begins an orderly life. A business manager maintains liquidity at the radio station, a housekeeper preserves cleanliness at home, and his love interest keeps his life uncomplicated by making no demands.

His life continues in this easy format until he approaches his fortieth birthday. Then he is suddenly struck by its emptiness, its lack of nobility. Instead of crisis or suffering, his days are filled with little more exciting than "nice people and a wonderful vinaigrette dressing" (16), his noblest venture being to host parties and try to get others to enjoy themselves. He tells Howard Freeman, a lawyer he meets in church, that he is a person "trapped in a good job" (17). That admission leads to radical changes in his life.

John, like Keillor himself, is enamored of sweet corn. John's father once called it one of the "four main pleasures of life" (108), and John shares his opinion, rhapsodizing when he thinks of eating fresh roasting ears with butter. Thus, when he gropes for something to give his life meaning, he clutches at memories of sweet corn and comes up with an idea for a farm restaurant. Its forte will be to grow fresh vegetables and serve them straight from the garden. Howard, as excited about the restaurant prospect as John, finds investors and draws up the necessary papers. Shortly after they find an appropriate farmhouse and get a bank loan, Howard brings in an acquaintance to do renovations. The project is just what John and Howard need to give purpose to their middle years . . . and perhaps to make them rich at the same time.

John's fortieth birthday party is attended by two people who also affect his life. One is Howard's sister Alida, a history professor who becomes John's lover. The other is a new dean whose goal for the radio station is the opposite of everything John has developed in his ten years of management. Dean Baird wants to change the radio programming from its concentration on classical music and National Public Radio news to all talk radio. John is perceptive enough to see that the dean's true motivation is not concern for minorities or the disadvantaged, groups he describes as being currently underrepresented; his driving force is a need to exercise power. He wants to make changes to show that he can.

To that end, he makes John hire a public affairs director who, in eighteen months, manages to produce only two documentary shows. One deals with premature menopause, and the other is an exposé on dental fillings that give people mercury poisoning. The latter, which receives a duPont award, John considers a "thoroughly mind-numbing piece of radio" (45). He unhesitatingly admits that he hates talk shows, particularly on public radio. All of the people who speak seem to be good people with progressive ideas, but they are all *"deeply concerned"* (45), and they spend the whole time trying to exhibit that concern. John considers the result "audio oatmeal, two hours of which isn't worth one Chopin Prelude" (45).

Because John is hoping the station will receive an endowment from a rich benefactor, he is not unduly worried by the dean's siege, and he turns his attention to other things. The restaurant project is not going well. It seems that Steve, the contractor, is both over budget and behind schedule. Steve thinks of himself as an artist instead of a carpenter and has commissioned a giant cornucopia for the dining room. What money he has not poured into the cornucopia he has wasted because of carelessness and mismanagement. When the restaurant does not open on schedule, the bank shows concern, but John assumes Howard will take care of the situation. Then Alida tells him Howard is "the unstable one" (36) in her family.

While attending the New York City funeral of a Lake Wobegon exile, John looks around at the thirty people there. He is struck by the emptiness of the inner life of this outwardly successful man and vows to fill his own emptiness by asking Alida to marry him. In fact, he is ready to give her a speech "about wanting a real life" (59) when she says, "I was thinking today: I finally got my life the way I want it. Don't you feel that way?" (59). Her comment so unnerves him that he suggests he go to New York City and become *her* wife, a proposal that seems made half in jest. He feels that she has tabled his marriage motion before he can even make it.

Most analysts agree that without conflict no real plot can exist. Thus writers introduce complications based on one or more basic conflicts. In just a few pages, Keillor adds three different complications to the plot. The most obvious is the job situation. John's job security is threatened because of a simple conflict between two persons, between the protagonist and the antagonist. The other complications, the restaurant project and the romance with Alida, both stem from the previously mentioned conflict, an internal struggle with himself.

It is significant that Lake Wobegon seldom enters the book until this point. John has successfully escaped the small town in which he grew up. He has developed habits and tastes far removed from his origins. During his easy years he makes biennial visits to Lake Wobegon but otherwise gives it little thought. However, once he starts his search for fulfilment, he returns again and again, in both thought and reality.

All of these visits are not as nostalgic as his memories of sweet corn. He can clearly see the faults of his hometown and the people who remain there. In his mind, if Alida does not marry him, it will be because she can see who he really is. That is the reason he has not taken her to Lake Wobegon. People there "believe that any display of learning is purely superficial, that nobody is smarter than anyone else" (63), not an attitude likely to endear them to a professor at Columbia University. He is afraid Alida will consider him just like all those people. "Different hairstyle, same head" (65).

Nevertheless, for most people home is a refuge, and so it is with John. The three complications of his life work together to send him scurrying back to Lake Wobegon. First, the worrisome debts of the restaurant keep mounting. Then Alida, who is doing research on a Danish companion to Susan B. Anthony, must spend her summer in Copenhagen. After she leaves, John is sorely tempted to resume a relationship with a former girlfriend. He resists, but the temptation remains. In addition, during Membership Week, the annual fund-raising period when public radio stations raise money for their programs by not airing them, a feminist reporter asks for an interview. It is clear from the questions she asks that her purpose is not to promote public radio but to discredit John for inadequately focusing on women's issues. Whether or not she has been encouraged by the new dean, John realizes her interview will undoubtedly work against him in his efforts to maintain current programming and his position.

John takes the first plane he can get and arrives unexpectedly in Lake Wobegon. His mother intuitively asks whether he is in any trouble. Although he admits he probably is, he tells her that is not why he is there; he has come to feel the reassurance of home. Unfortunately, what he mostly feels is overwhelmed. His father Byron, always a packrat, has time to attend auctions now that he has retired. John attributes his search for bargains to his Lutheran upbringing, but Byron overdoes it. If he spots humidifiers at a good price, he buys several whether or not he needs even one. He stockpiles army ammunition boxes, antique half-penny nails, and air filters for automobiles he no longer owns. The garage is jammed with "old tools with broken handles waiting for the tool

resurrection" (190). The basement and attic are overflowing with his accumulated finds while all the rooms in the house are "under serious
siege" (81). John is dismayed by the unremitting clutter of the family
home and equally disturbed by the clutter of family gossip about relatives with assorted problems. He finally has to leave the house to get
fresh air and a fresh perspective.

After eating lunch at the Chatterbox Cafe, he strolls down Main Street,
past the Norwegian bachelor farmers sitting in front of Ralph's Pretty
Good Grocery, and on to the Lutheran parsonage to see his sister Judy
Ingqvist. She does not share his concern about their father, and he feels
somewhat rebuffed, remembering how close he and Judy were when
they were at the university and how that closeness shattered when she
married the Lutheran minister. John thinks of David Ingqvist as Mr.
Vanilla and finds Judy's present role as minister's wife a distinct short-
fall, not what she should have achieved as the smartest one in the family.

Nevertheless, the visit to Judy sets his mind going in another direction.
The Ingqvists built their garage with boards from the ancestral Tollefson
house. The original John Tollefson, the great-grandfather after whom the
protagonist is named, was a lighthearted young man not easily dismayed
by the roadblocks put in the way of his emigration to America. His father
scorned the idea and insisted that he marry the butcher's daughter in
his native Voss, Norway. He obeyed, and the newlyweds joined the
butcher's household. John carefully avoided offending his in-laws, who
were humorless pietists, and told them nothing of his dreams of the New
World. He shared them with his wife, however, and convinced her that
they should go as soon as he could save the money. He finally earned
it through a wager that took desperate courage and some chicanery. John
heard the story when he was small, and he takes strength from it as he
recalls it now.

When John returns to New York, he feels "reconfigured for fidelity"
(105), but his other problems remain. Calls to the woman from whom
he was expecting an endowment reach an answering service; the dean
remains adversarial; Howard, the managing partner of the restaurant
investment, is elusive. After John finally tracks him down, Howard admits the bank can do what it likes with the restaurant because the partners are nine months behind in making their loan payments. When John
reacts with incredulity, Howard retreats from reality.

Nonetheless, these problems all pale in comparison to the newspaper
article that awaits him when he returns from accepting an award in

Washington. The reporter who interviewed him has a feature article on the front page of the *Syracuse Reader*. In it she accuses him of having difficulty working with assertive women, of fostering a business climate in which women are afraid to voice their opinions. He is accused of getting drunk, of groping women, and of telling jokes that belittle them. Written in the best tradition of tabloid journalism, the article makes assertions based on a grain of truth. He actually did tell the joke quoted although whether it belittles anyone is questionable. A photo of him holding a wine glass accompanies the article. What hurts John the most is that it was taken by a guest at one of his parties. People who enjoyed his hospitality are now knifing him in the back, both maligning his character and denigrating his management of WSJO.

John's reactions to the article come in stages. First is disappointment in those with whom he has worked for so many years. Whether or not they had any notion of the reporter's hidden agenda, they contributed to the article. John's second reaction is to type a letter to the paper complaining that the article is composed entirely of lies and perversions of the truth. It is a good letter, but he destroys it. Next, he writes to Alida comparing himself to hybrid tomatoes developed for long shelf life. He tells her that they are not real tomatoes but semblances of tomatoes. In the same way he is not a person but a semblance of a person. He wants to do something noble like marry her and have children. He deletes that letter too.

Alida, having returned from Denmark, is busy editing her book. John dreams of her getting a job in the history department of his college and then realizes that such a situation is as unrealistic as is his remaining much longer at the radio station. His attempts at finding a job in New York City turn up only one offer—to sell shoes. His life remains in limbo until Thanksgiving. Then, at Alida's suggestion, he invites his parents to come for the holidays. His mother is eager to meet Alida and convinces Byron to come even though he considers Lake Wobegon the only sane place to be and has no idea why anyone would leave it.

The holiday visit is a resounding success. John's mother Mary and Alida like each other immediately. Byron is exhausted and nervous from two days of hard driving and immediately wanders all over the house asking impertinent questions and putting down everything from John's taste to his politics. Yet after dinner and several glasses of wine and champagne, he begins to mellow, and John sees a new side of his father. Byron asks Alida if she has ever heard of privy-tipping, explaining that it is part of American history, her specialty. He then launches into stories of his own experiences with the sport, stories John has never heard. Byron warms toward Alida, who finds both parents delightful.

The turning point in the novel comes in January when Byron dies. His death is entirely unexpected. Coming up from the basement, he sits down on a step to catch his breath, and dies with a package of frozen peas in his hand. John, of course, leaves immediately for Minnesota. His siblings and an uncle are there before him, and the reader gets to meet them all. The surprise comes when Alida walks in just before the funeral. All unbeknownst to John, she has flown to Minneapolis and driven through the snow to arrive in time for the service. Her boldness inspires the same quality in John, and finally, after the funeral is over and the wake, he finds the courage to ask Alida to marry him, and she accepts.

Most of the complications proceed to their inevitable conclusions. The restaurant deal collapses, and the possibility of a bequest to underwrite classical programming is lost when the donor dies. With the dean's triumph imminent, John resigns as manager of the station. Nevertheless, for him the most important conflict has turned out all right. He marries Alida, who is still teaching at Columbia, and settles into a flat in New York City happily playing the role that he once suggested in jest, that of house husband.

Marriage is the traditional ending to comedy. After overcoming seemingly unsurmountable difficulties, the romantic love interests finally get together, and all is well. *Wobegon Boy*, however, is not a traditional comedy. John is not able to overcome all his difficulties. The humor in the novel comes from the excesses of human nature which, laughable though they may be, do triumph. Nevertheless, John has fulfilled his quest. He has seen marriage and potential family as necessary to give his life purpose, and he has achieved his goal. The other complications of his life pale by comparison.

CHARACTER DEVELOPMENT

Garrison Keillor has created more complex characters in *Wobegon Boy* than in all his previous writing put together. In addition to John Tollefson, the first-person protagonist whose story the book tells, three characters are memorable—John's father, his mother, and his lover Alida.

Byron Tollefson, John's father, is a complicated individual whom John has never understood. As a boy, Byron did not get along with his own father and went to live with his Uncle Svend, who gave him a horse. John realizes the only time he ever heard Byron speak of love was in connection with that horse. Riding it made the shy boy, always an outsider at school, feel proud. Then the horse got into some oats, became bloated, and had to be put to sleep. When he could not reach the veterinarian, Byron had to shoot her himself.

The fortitude Byron showed in that incident as a youth has sustained him through life. It enabled him to persist in wooing Mary when she had been dating a wealthy and suave young man, and it has helped him to survive later ordeals. However, the unexpected incident with the horse contributed to an increasingly dark outlook. He has always expected the worst, and as he gets older, he increasingly tries to prepare for it. He covers his house with signs, such as Door to Bathroom Is Behind You—This Is Closet, and stockpiles thirty-seven packages of Jimmy Dean sausage in the freezer. In John's opinion, the excessive or useless articles, acquired as a hedge against disaster, eventually become his father's attempt to forestall death.

Constant worry keeps Byron thin and nervous. During his two years as a scoutmaster, he overdid the Boy Scout motto "Be Prepared" and so fretted on camping trips that the scouts were relieved when his term was up. Whatever disaster could befall, from bears to tetanus to lost boys, he was sure would occur on his watch. In his later years he continues to express such vigilance, fearing to leave his home in case the plumbing might leak, the furnace go out. When he visits John, he asks how much his house cost, searches the ceiling for water stains, and wonders if something is wrong with a floor covered with wall-to-wall carpeting. What John characterizes as fault-finding seems in fact consistent with Byron's constant hunt for pitfalls that can pose a problem for him or any member of his family. His incessant activity bothers John, who is uncomfortable being around him for very long.

During his active years, Byron ran the grain elevator. He led the Fourth of July celebration, organizing its living flag demonstration. In retirement he continues his community involvement by serving on the town council and taking charge of flooding the ice-skating rink. His responsibility to family and community is beyond question, but tributes at his funeral surprise John. When Clarence Bunsen tells how Byron tried to get senior citizen housing started in Lake Wobegon, John is taken aback even though the idea is consistent with the need to prepare for the inevitable. Then, when the mayor characterizes Byron as a peacemaker on the town council, John realizes he is hearing about a side of his father he never saw. He wonders, "Who is this wonderful man people keep telling me about?" (235). He wonders what happened to the father who accumulated junk and was never satisfied with anything his son did.

At the wake someone comments that Byron was very proud of John, that he always talked about him. All John can reply is "I wish he'd told me" (243). Personal communication and sharing of emotion seem to be difficult for Tollefson males. John recognizes that he has the same problem with affection as his father, who "was always turning away" (171). After Byron dies, John desperately wishes he had shown his father more affection, but he thinks that had he hugged his father, Byron would have had a heart attack. It is John's mother who tells him his father thought highly of his children; Byron could never bring himself to say so.

In most respects Mary Tollefson is the opposite of her husband. She takes everything in stride. When she was young, she lost her sister to scarlet fever, and her father lost his farm in a drought, but she remained undaunted. She loved dancing and fast cars, and despite her family's poverty, she was popular with both young men and young women. For a year she dated a Yale student whose father owned a department store in St. Cloud. Yet practicality is another of her characteristics. She could see something in his nature that anticipated his eventually running that store into the ground, and when he proposed, she refused. The practicality continues to the end. She cooks the peas Byron was holding when he died. To her daughter Diana's objections she replies, "He touched everything in this house. . . . What's the problem?" (167).

Mary is not happy when the Sons of Knute ask to participate in the funeral service. She considers the fraternal organization, with its swords and capes and plumes, an attempt at swashbuckling. Nevertheless, she is resilient enough to allow a modified rite in which they tap the coffin of the deceased and say, "Go straight home" (193). A basically kind person, Mary can not refuse their request to say good-bye in a way that is meaningful to them if somewhat silly to others. She can no more offend the Sons of Knute than she can chide Byron about his accumulated treasures, attempting to curb his acquisitiveness by suggestion rather than by confrontation. She has genuine affection for Byron, her children, and others, but she is not sentimental. As soon as Byron dies, she gets rid of his junk in near record time, and she waits only a few months before accepting a dinner invitation from her former beau, now a widower. When Diana asks to wear her wedding dress but is too large for it, Mary rips it up so that she can make a jacket from the skirt.

Perhaps Mary's most important characteristic is her unfailing common sense. She chooses to bury Byron in what he wore when he was happiest, his work clothes. Her sister-in-law wonders what people will say, but Mary responds that people had a whole lifetime to look down on him. If that is what they want to do, she sees no reason why they would wait until the funeral. Likewise, when John tells her he and Alida are not sure they will be successful at marriage, she quietly comments, "Oh, there's no such thing as a successful marriage. . . . There are marriages that give up and marriages that keep on trying, that's the only difference" (142).

Alida Freeman, the woman whom John does indeed marry, is an equally interesting character. When he first meets her, John is taken by her obvious likes and dislikes, with more of the latter. Each day she takes two showers, smokes two cigarettes, and drinks a glass of wine. She dislikes background music and cannot stand public pedicures or even the thought of nose-picking. John thinks she may be a bit self-centered, but he immediately knows her to be the love of his life.

The reader discovers that Alida is a hard-working academic who is serious about both her teaching and her research. She has managed to get hired at Columbia, an Ivy League school noted for its high standards, and she thrives in that setting. John may dream of her getting a job at his college, but the thought of giving up her current position never occurs to Alida. She is an independent woman, although not the militant feminist her mother was. In fact, she gets hissed when she speaks on a panel in Chicago and says women of her generation are not obsessed with anger at men, that they do not blame men for everything that goes wrong in their lives.

There is a strong physical attraction between Alida and John, and she is as eager for their time together as he. They settle into a routine of seeing each other every other weekend, alternating between her apartment in New York City and his house in Red Cliff. For a while that seems to satisfy them both. Then John decides that their arrangement, even though it is the envy of their friends, is not enough, yet he cannot bring himself to propose. When he finally gets the courage, she tells him that she now has her life the way she wants it. He takes that as a rejection before he can make the offer, but he forgets that Alida brought up the idea of marriage earlier. At that time John said he was not sure he even believed in marriage. Now her statement is a defensive one. Just as people convince themselves that they do not really want something they cannot have, Alida says she does not want something she thinks he will never offer. Her later unhesitating acceptance of his proposal makes that clear.

John's initial appraisal of Alida, that she is a bit self-centered, turns out to be incorrect. Her trip to Byron's funeral reveals selflessness, and her ready acceptance of Byron and Mary indicates generosity. She has both determination and ambition, but neither gets in the way of her relationships with John or his family. It is she who asks why, if John loves her, she has not met his family. Her underlying values give strength to the relationship before she and John marry and should help that marriage survive after it takes place.

THEMATIC ISSUES

In *Wobegon Boy*, Garrison Keillor combines major themes with satire on various subjects. Rather than include short pieces of satire as he has done in previous books, he incorporates the satire into the novel. Most prominent among his targets are the jargon of higher education, the pretension of some National Public Radio offerings, and the pseudo-psychological lingo of New Age therapy and religion.

A satirist usually exaggerates a flaw in character or practice, but most of Keillor's objects of ridicule need no exaggeration. In giving Alida's academic credentials, Keillor mentions that she has moved quickly up the career ladder in her chosen field of nineteenth-century American history, eclipsing those scholars writing about "herstories," hermeneutics, deconstruction, or progressive revisionism. In recent years these topics have actually been among the most popular for doctoral dissertations.

Because National Public Radio need not appeal to advertisers, it can feature in-depth discussions, lectures, and interviews rarely presented on commercial radio. Such features serve listeners by providing both deeper insight and broader perspective on any given topic. Nevertheless, occasionally there will be someone like Jonah Hadley, whom Keillor depicts as a regular on NPR's *All Things Considered*. In his weekly journal, Hadley throws together such diverse references as the quest for the Holy Grail, the myth of Sisyphus, African-American heritage, Alexis de Tocqueville, and a Sufi poet. His whole purpose is to impress rather than impart knowledge, and the point of his references eludes even the most erudite listener. Again Keillor does not have to amplify anything about such a speaker, but he does exaggerate when he gives the titles of the talk shows that will replace classical music on WSJO. Even the most dedicated devotees of off-the-wall causes would find little similarity between any groups they support and those allotted fifteen minutes under the dean's new talk-only format. Shows such as *People in Search of Closure*,

People in Grief for Former Lovers, and the *Herpes Hour* provide humor at the same time that they show the absurdity of the dean's proposal.

Psychobabble is one of Keillor's favorite targets. He has written many short pieces making fun of talk that sounds authoritative and means nothing. He adds it here in connection with John's sister Diana and her partner. The two women meet at a seminar given by a former heroin addict who has found an easy way to make himself rich. Entitled "Changing Your Life Story Through Positive Projection," the seminar has as its main point that "the search for answers is itself a valid answer" (185). Here again, to get the satirical effect he wants, Keillor need only present the kind of talk one can find readily in publications espousing self-help and renewal. No overstatement is necessary.

Practitioners of religious babble can sound even sillier than those who spout psychological babble. Keillor uses only one example—Mother Sally, the rector of the college chapel. The Gospel of John, sometimes called "The Book of Signs," has been studied by generations of Bible scholars. In the King James translation, the gospel begins, "In the beginning was the Word, and the Word was with God, and the Word was God." The great dramatist Johann Wolfgang von Goethe shows his title character Faust struggling to accurately translate that first verse. Faust variously interprets the Greek word *logos* as "word," "mind," "power," and "deed," all of which can be correct meanings, though not necessarily in that context. Mother Sally does not struggle, however. She glibly declares that "the Word is Womb, and the Womb is the Word" (10) and preaches her sermons on "energetic uteruses" (109).

All of the satire adds fun to the book, but the themes Keillor incorporates are serious. One of the themes is universal. Some thinkers divide the world into two kinds of people—those who see a glass as half empty and those who see it as half full. Others divide people into pessimists and optimists. Garrison Keillor divides Lake Wobegon residents into Dark Lutherans and Happy Lutherans.

John Tollefson sees the division in his own family. His mother is a Happy Lutheran like his namesake, the original John Tollefson. However, his paternal great-grandmother Signe was a Dark Lutheran, and the Tollefson descendants have all taken after her. In fact, most people in Lake Wobegon are Dark Lutherans. John explains the division. Dark Lutherans or Pietists belong to the Hauge Synod, which holds that people are utterly depraved. The Happy Lutherans, members of the Old Synod, are more relaxed about fundamental beliefs and particularly about human nature. These synodical divisions are based on fact. The

Hauge Synod originated in Norway, and immigrants brought its beliefs with them to this country where they are alive and well.

The Hauge belief that people are basically evil makes Keillor's Dark Lutherans unduly worried and suspicious. In addition, they suffer from an extreme portion of guilt for which they have no easy method of atonement. They cannot go to confession like Catholics. Instead they must find other ways to expiate their sin, like committee work or volunteer jobs. John opines, "Your average peewee-hockey coach is a guy who is paying back for a weekend in a motel with an aerobics instructor named Trish" (202).

The second and most important theme has to do with the small-town legacy. Like many a person who grew up in a small town, John Tollefson initially sees only the down side of Lake Wobegon and its inhabitants. He is particularly dismayed by the self-satisfaction and the lack of ambition or curiosity. The town proverb seems to be "Life is complicated so think small" (3). People prefer to be in the audience rather than on the stage, and they condemn those who desire to excel whether because of appearance, intelligence, or talent. Because John is intrigued by the outside world the locals regard with suspicion, his condemnation of those in his hometown is natural. Only later can he look beyond the bad points to the good.

It takes maturity to discern the strength, the sense of continuity that is present in small towns in which people stay put for generation after generation, where they know and care for one another. John senses this when he realizes that his life lacks focus. He thinks marriage and family will give him the sense of purpose he lacks. In fact, it is his father who sums it up: "The stream of insults that life directs at you cannot be vanquished by skill or cunning. . . . The only answer is to be loved so that nothing else matters so much" (292). This is the conclusion John himself reaches by the end of the book.

ALTERNATE READING: NEW CRITICISM

New Criticism, one of the most popular of all critical approaches, actually began as a reaction to approaches that preceded it. In the first part of the twentieth century, biographical and historical critics concentrated on analyzing the relationship between a work of literature and the life of its creator or the political, social, and economic events concurrent with the time of its creation.

The pioneers of New Criticism asserted that a literary work should be judged on its own merit; its meaning should not be determined by external factors. Their ideas began emerging in the 1920s but were not given a name until 1941 when John Crowe Ransom published *The New Criticism*. In that book he pulled together the theories of various critics and in the process laid down a critical methodology still used by many educators today. Ransom held that a literary work, like a musical score, can be taken apart to discover its true meaning "independent of its author's intention, or the emotional state, or the values and beliefs of either its author or reader" (Bressler 38).

Instead of considering the author's life, the historical context, or a reader's emotional response, New Critics do a close reading in which they look at the title, components, and organization of a poem or other literary work. They consider both denotative and connotative meanings of individual words. They address symbolism and imagery. They think about tone. Then they put these elements together by considering relationships. For instance, are there any paradoxes? Any ambiguities? If so, is the tone ironic? By analyzing those elements that have tension, that do not seem to go together, analysts can go on to appraise those qualities that unify and resolve the ambiguities, such as theme. In that way they can decipher the true import of the text.

Although New Criticism is most effective with poetry, it can also be used with fiction. A close reading of *Wobegon Boy* can illuminate the central conflict and reveal meaning. John Tollefson's first-person narration begins with homely bits of wisdom from his early life in Lake Wobegon. Most of the wisdom comes from his mother, who adjures him to be happy, be polite, and avoid self-pity. He attributes her advice partly to her sunny disposition and ability to look on the bright side, but also partly to location. In Minnesota everyone is equally cold. Anyone who takes his or her discomfort personally will not last long in that climate.

For all the validity of his mother's instruction, John wants nothing more than to get away from the small town. He yearns for the sophistication of a life in which people of taste not only know about art, music, and literature but also know what wine to order with what entree. He finds that life, and for ten years enjoys a style of living characterized by good taste and comfort.

Until his fortieth birthday, his life is spent leaving Lake Wobegon behind. Once he successfully escapes, his visits there are made from filial duty only. Then several crises precipitate a search for meaning in his life, for nobility and purpose. That search eventually takes him back to Lake

Wobegon, not geographically but philosophically. There he finds peace in the wisdom his mother imparted to him when he was young. As he drives away from his home in Red Cliff to his new life in New York City, he realizes that people in the towns he passes are very like those in Lake Wobegon. They too try to do the best with what they have, and when they do, things turn out all right.

The paradox is that John Tollefson ends where he begins, but astute readers will not be surprised by that. They will have noticed that the title is *Wobegon Boy*. In a sense, John is always a son of Lake Wobegon. Try as he may, he never completely leaves his upbringing behind; he just masks it and ignores it until life's vicissitudes point out the necessity of returning to core values.

Study of the denotative and connotative meanings of individual words is less important in a novel than in poetry, but examination of the title and the tensions in construction are important in both. A close reading of any novel can illuminate the theme and enhance understanding as it does in *Wobegon Boy*.

Bibliography

WORKS BY GARRISON KEILLOR

"The Bangor Man." *The New Yorker*, October 14, 1972, 39.

The Book of Guys. New York: Viking, 1993.

"The Boy Who Couldn't Have TV." *TV Guide*, May 15, 1982, 39–42.

Cat, You Better Come Home. New York: Viking, 1995.

"A Christmas Story." *The New Yorker*, December 25, 1989, 40–42.

"The Chuck Show." *The New Yorker*, July 24, 1989, 26–29.

"Drop Dead, Lewis Carroll: History's Rejection Slips." *The New York Times Book Review*, May 1, 1994, 3+.

"Get Ready for Monday Night Mudwrestling." *TV Guide*, December 7, 1985, 5–6.

G. K. the DJ. St. Paul: Minnesota Public Radio, 1977.

Happy to Be Here. New York: Atheneum, 1981.

Happy to Be Here. Rev. ed. New York: Penguin, 1983.

"He Digests the Star and Finds It's a Meat-and-Potatoes Meal." *Minneapolis Star*, August 4, 1977, 1–2C.

"How the Savings and Loans Were Saved." *The New Yorker*, October 16, 1989, 42.

"If Begonias Bloom, Can Baseball Be Far Behind?" *Minneapolis Tribune*, April 1, 1979, A17.

"In Autumn We All Get Older Again." *Time*, November 6, 1995, 90.

"Intriguers." *People Weekly*, December 28, 1987, 82–83.

"It's Good Old Monogamy That's Really Sexy." *Time*, October 17, 1994, 71.

"A Lake Wobegon Christmas—Such Were the Joys." *The New York Times Book Review*, December 8, 1985, 7.

Lake Wobegon Days. New York: Viking, 1985.

"Lake Wobegon Days." *The Atlantic Monthly*, August 1985, 27–43.

Leaving Home: A Collection of Lake Wobegon Stories. New York: Viking, 1987.

"Lonesome Shorty." *The New Yorker*, March 5, 1990, 36–37.

"Lust on Wheels." *Esquire*, July 1986, 61.

"Midnight Meeting about Secret Meetings." *Minneapolis Star*, March 13, 1979, 4A.

"A Most Unflattering Show." *Time*, March 13, 1995, 96.

"My Son, the Delivery Entrepreneur." *Minneapolis Star*, January 25, 1979, A6.

"O Baby, Baby." *Time*, April 13, 1998, 232.

The Old Man Who Loved Cheese. Boston: Little, Brown, 1996.

"Onward and Upward with the Arts: At the Opry." *The New Yorker*, May 6, 1974, 46–70.

"The Poetry Judge." *The Atlantic Monthly*, February 1996, 93–96.

"St. Paul Orchestra's Pure Sunshine." *Minneapolis Tribune*, January 27, 1974, A11.

"Sex Tips." *The New Yorker*, August 14, 1971, 31.

"Snack Firm Maps New Chip Push." *The New Yorker*, October 10, 1970, 45.

"Some Matters Concerning the Occupant." *The Atlantic Monthly*, July 1968, 54.

"Sweet Home, Minnesota." *Time*, March 24, 1997, 108.

"Three New Twins Join Club in Spring." *The New Yorker*, February 22, 1988, 32–33.

"Toasting the Flag." *New York Times*, July 2, 1989, E13.

"Voices of Liberty." *Newsweek*, July 14, 1986, 33.

"Who's on the Right Track?" *Minneapolis Tribune*, January 14, 1974, A8.

"With All the Trimmings." *Time*, November 27, 1995, 108.

"You Say Potato." *Time*, April 22, 1996, 100.

We Are Still Married: Stories and Letters. New York: Viking, 1989.

WLT: A Radio Romance. New York: Viking, 1991.

Wobegon Boy. New York: Viking, 1997.

Geng, Veronica, and Garrison Keillor. "A Good Man Is Hard to Keep: The Correspondence of Flannery O'Connor and S. J. Perelman." *The New York Times Book Review*, April 2, 1995, 15–16.

WORKS ABOUT GARRISON KEILLOR

General Information and Criticism

Austin, Jonathan D. "Through It All, Host of 'A Prairie Home Companion' Is a Writer." *CNN Interactive*, November 25, 1998. Accessed February 6, 1999 at: ⟨http://www.cnn.com/books/news/9811/25/garrison.keillor/index.html⟩

Barsamian, David. "The Gloomy View from Lake Wobegon." *The Nation*, January 5, 1998:10.

Bunzel, Reed E. "Garrison Keillor: An American Radio Romance." *Broadcasting*, January 6, 1992, 86–87.

Coleman, Nick. "Preaching the Gospel According to Garrison." *Minnesota Star and Tribune*, July 1, 1984, 1G+.

Damsker, Matt. "Heartland Humor Flows from Depths of Wobegon." *The San Diego Union*, March 6, 1983, E1+.

Fisher, Marc. "Constant Companion." *Washington Post*, June 14, 1998, F1+.

Fiske, Edward. "A Humorist Who Celebrates Small-Town America." *New York Times*, October 31, 1982, H23C.

Foss, Sonja K., and Karen A. Foss. "The Construction of Feminine Spectatorship in Garrison Keillor's Radio Monologues." *Quarterly Journal of Speech* 80 (1994): 410–26.

Healey, Barth. "Sex and Violence in Wobegon." *The New York Times Book Review*, August 25, 1985, 15.

Heim, David. "Garrison Keillor and Culture Protestantism." *The Christian Century* 104 (1987): 517–19.

Hertzberg, Hendrik. "Cross Talk." *The New Republic*, August 22, 1988, 42.

Holston, Noel. "Keillor Sounds Less 'Wobegon,' More World-Weary." *Minneapolis Star Tribune*, July 4, 1999, F4.

———. "Longtime 'Companion.' " *Minneapolis Star Tribune*, July 4, 1999, F1+.

Klose, Kevin. "The Keillor Instinct for the Truer-Than-True." *Washington Post*, September 15, 1985, K1+.

"Lake Wobegon and Other Literary Landscapes." *Life*, January 1986, 116+.

Langway, Lynn, and Sylvester Monroe. "Meeting the Gang at Lake Wobegon." *Newsweek*, December 7, 1981, 106+.

Larson, Charles U., and Christine Oravec. "*A Prairie Home Companion* and the Fabrication of Community." *Critical Studies in Mass Communication* 4 (1987): 221–44.

Pederson-Pietersen, Laura. "From Lake Wobegon and Beyond, a Round Table on Economics and Finance." *New York Times*, February 3, 1995, 4BU.

Plimpton, George. "Garrison Keillor, the Art of Humor II." *Paris Review* 37.136(1995): 109–27.

"Radio Is 'a Magical Country.' " *U. S. News & World Report*, November 4, 1985, 75.

Sanoff, Alvin P. "New and Old Voices Put the Snap Back into Radio." *U. S. News & World Report*, November 4, 1985, 74.

Scholl, Peter. "Garrison Keillor and the News from Lake Wobegon." *Studies in American Humor* ns 4(1985–86): 217–28.

Schreffler, Peter H. " 'Where All the Children Are Above Average': Garrison Keillor as a Model for Personal Narrative Assignments." *College Composition and Communication* 40(1989): 82–85.

Steele, Mike. "KSJN: Giant Step for Public Broadcasting?" *Minneapolis Tribune*, November 15, 1970, E1+.

Sussman, Vic. "How Guys Live Their Lives." *U. S. News & World Report*, November 15, 1993, 77.

Vecsey, George. "Manhattan As a Bit of Prairie." *New York Times*, November 29, 1996, C1+.

Viles, Peter. "Thoughts from Lake Wobegone [sic] on the Superhighway." *Broadcasting & Cable*, January 10, 1994, 56–58.

Wall, James M. "The Secret Is Out about Lake Wobegon." *The Christian Century*, November 13, 1985, 1019–20.

Wilbers, Stephen. "Lake Wobegon: Mythical Place and the American Imagination." *American Studies* 30(1989): 5–21.

Biographical Information

"ABA to Underwrite Keillor Radio Series." *Publishers Weekly*, December 23, 1988, 17.

Baenen, Jeff. "Keillor Still Adds Splash of Color to World of Talk." *Johnson City Press*, December 18, 1997, 15.

Barol, Bill. "A Shy Person Says So Long." *Newsweek*, June 15, 1987, 65–66.

———. "What Now, Wobegon?" *Newsweek*, October 5, 1987, 82–83.

Barron, James. "Writer's Cramp." *New York Times*, September 17, 1998, B2.

Beyette, Beverly. "Fishing for Meaning in Lake Wobegon Waters." *Los Angeles Times*, September 18, 1985, V1–3.

Bolick, Katie. "It's Just Work." *Atlantic Unbound*, October 8, 1997. Accessed February 6, 1999 at: ⟨http://www.theatlantic.com/unbound/factfict/gkint.htm⟩

Bowermaster, Jon. "Fresh Voices Hope to Be Far from Lake Wobegon." *New York Times*, December 13, 1987, H43+.

Bream, Jon. "Garrison Keillor: A Decade of 'Prairie Home Companion.' " *Minneapolis Star and Tribune*, July 1, 1984: 4–13.

Bromberg, Craig. "Live from Brooklyn, It's . . . Garrison Keillor." *Wall Street Journal*, March 22, 1990, A12.

Bunce, Alan. "From a Town 'That Time Forgot,' Master Folklorist Keillor." *Christian Science Monitor*, September 6, 1985, 1+.

Close, Roy M. "Humorist, Poet Create Show That at Best Is Wildly Funny." *Minneapolis Star*, January 5, 1974, A10.

"Coffee and Minnows." *The Economist*, September 16, 1989, 96.

Fedo, Michael. *The Man from Lake Wobegon*. New York: St. Martin's, 1987.

Galant, Debbie. "A Lost 'Companion.' " *New York*, June 15, 1987, 25.

"Garrison Keillor." Online posting. *A Prairie Home Companion*. Accessed January 10, 1998 at: ⟨http://phc.mpr.org/cast/garrison_keillor.shtml⟩.

"Garrison Keillor: An American Home Companion." *Broadcasting*, December 15, 1986, 127.

"Garrison Keillor Falls Prey to N.Y. Tabloid Gossip." *St. Paul Pioneer Press*, November 16, 1991, 11A+.

"Garrison Keillor's Surprising Surge." *U. S. News & World Report*, October 5, 1998, 12.

Graham, S. Keith. "Keillor Finds His Way Through Big-city Show." *Atlanta Constitution*, May 25, 1990: DO2.

Halvorsen, Donna. "Keillor Tips His Hat to Anoka, a Place He Says He Never Really Left." *Minneapolis Star Tribune*, June 5, 1990: 1B.

Hemingson, Peter. "The Plowboy Interview: Garrison Keillor: The Voice of Lake Wobegon." *Mother Earth News*, May-June 1985, 17+."

Hertzberg, Hendrik. "Washington Diarist." *The New Republic*, August 22, 1988, 42.

"A Home Companion Bids Farewell." *Broadcasting*, June 22, 1987, 39–40.

Ingrassia, Lawrence. "Live from St. Paul, Here's 'A Prairie Home Companion.' " *Wall Street Journal*, January 21, 1981, 1+.

Jones, Will. "After Last Night." *Minneapolis Tribune*, October 3, 1971, 6D; October 9, 1971, 10A; October 31, 1971, 4D.

"Keillor Re-ups with MPR, 26 New ARCA Shows Planned." *Broadcasting*, May 21, 1990, 63–64.

"Keillor to Quit Daily Show; Others Leave KSJN." *Minneapolis Tribune*, August 24, 1973, B14.

"Keillor, Wife Welcome New Daughter." *Johnson City Press*, January 2, 1998, 13.

Kling, William. "Farewell to Lake Wobegon." *U. S. News & World Report*, June 22, 1987, 10.

Lague, Louise. "Garrison Keillor: Favorite Son of the Town Time Forgot." *People Weekly*, February 6, 1984, 42–44.

"Lake Wobegon's Garrison Keillor Finds a Love That Time Forgot and the Decades Can't Improve." *People Weekly*, November 25, 1985, 62.

Lee, Judith Yaross. *Garrison Keillor, a Voice of America*. Jackson: University Press of Mississippi, 1991.

Letofsky, Irv. "For Garrison Keillor, Fantasy Is a Lot More Fun than Reality." *Minneapolis Tribune*, July 29, 1976, C1+.

Levin, Eric. "Goodbye to Lake Wobegon: Garrison Keillor, the Author of *Leaving Home*, Is Doing Just That." *People Weekly*, October 12, 1987, 34–37.

"A Little Girl Is Born" Online posting. *A Prairie Home Companion*. Accessed January 10, 1998 at: ⟨http://phc.mpr.org/activities/little/⟩.

MacDonald, Gordon. "Lake Wobegon's Prodigal Son." *Christianity Today*, May 18, 1992, 33–35.

Martin, Douglas. "From Lake Wobegon to the Hudson." *New York Times*, December 14, 1987, B1+.

McDowell, Edwin. "Keillor on Radio." *New York Times*, October 11, 1989, C22.

McGrath, Anne. "Eye on Publishing." *Wilson Library Bulletin* 60.3(1985): 32–33.

Meier, Peg. "Seeking Obscurity Again in Denmark." *Minneapolis Star and Tribune,* March 22, 1987, 1A+.

Nelson, Tim, and Mark Stansbury. "Keillor Show Coming Home." *St. Paul Pioneer Press,* March 29, 1992, 1A+.

Newlund, Sam. "Ingenuity Helps Keillor Take Crassness out of Christmas." *Minneapolis Star and Tribune,* December 15, 1982, 13T.

"Portrait: Garrison Keillor." *Life,* May 1982, 27–32.

" 'Prairie Home' Is Closed for Good." *Broadcasting,* February 23, 1987, 70.

"Public Radio's Programming Explosion." *Broadcasting,* May 29, 1989, 57–58.

Radel, Cliff. "Home on the Prairie." *The Cincinnati Enquirer,* March 4, 1982, B9+.

"Return of an Above-Average Broadcaster." *U. S. News & World Report,* May 29, 1989, 12.

Roback, Diane. "Leaving the Shores of Lake Wobegon." *Publishers Weekly,* August 21, 1987, 34–35.

———. *"PW* Interviews Garrison Keillor." *Publishers Weekly,* September 13, 1985, 138–39.

Rothstein, Mervyn. "Keillor Remembers the 'Town That Time Forgot.' " *New York Times,* August 20, 1985, C20.

Scholl, Peter A. "Garrison Keillor." *Dictionary of Literary Biography Yearbook.* Detroit: Gale, 1988. 326–38.

———. *Garrison Keillor.* New York: Twayne, 1993.

Schumacher, Michael. "Sharing the Laughter with Garrison Keillor." *Writer's Digest,* January 1986, 32–35.

Skow, John. "Leaving Lake Wobegon: Garrison Keillor Closes Down a Unique Radio Show." *Time,* June 29, 1987, 64–65.

———. "Lonesome Whistle Blowing." *Time,* November 4, 1985, 68–73.

———. "Wild Seed in the Big Apple." *Time,* December 11, 1989, 109.

Sutin, Lawrence. "Lake Wobegon: the Town That Time Forgot; Where Women Are Strong, the Men Good-looking, and the Children Above Average." *Saturday Evening Post,* September 1986, 42+.

Thorpe, Doug. "Garrison Keillor's 'Prairie Home Companion': Gospel of the Airwaves." *The Christian Century,* July 21–28, 1982, 1793–96.

"What's Up at Lake Wobegon." *Time,* November 9, 1981, 95.

REVIEWS AND CRITICISM

Happy to Be Here

Review of *Happy to Be Here. People Weekly,* February 22, 1982, 20.

Mano, D. Keith. "Here at the New Yorker." *National Review,* December 11, 1981, 1492.

Skow, John. "Main Street's Shy Revisionist." *Time,* February 1, 1982, 74.

Lake Wobegon Days

Forbes, Malcolm S. Review of *Lake Wobegon Days*. *Forbes*, February 10, 1986, 19.

Geng, Veronica. "Idylls of Minnesota." *The New York Times Book Review*, August 25, 1985, 1+.

Review of *Lake Wobegon Days*. *The New Yorker*, October 7, 1985, 140.

Michelson, Bruce. "Keillor and Rölvaag and the Art of Telling the Truth." *American Studies*, 30.1 (1989): 21–34.

Miller, William Lee. "*Solo Gratia* in Lake Wobegon." *The Christian Century*, November 13, 1985, 1019–20.

Reed, J. D. "Home, Home on the Strange." *Time*, September 2, 1985, 70.

Youngren, J. Alan. "The News from Lake Wobegon." *Christianity Today*, November 22, 1985, 33–36.

Leaving Home

Anderson, A. J. Review of *Leaving Home*. *Library Journal*, October 1, 1987, 108.

Gray, Spalding. "Plenty Wholesome and a Little Perverse." *The New York Times Book Review*, October 4, 1987, 9.

Heim, David. "Keillor Cultivates a Natural Piety." *The Christian Century* 105 (1988): 126–29.

Schickel, Richard. "Just a Few Minutes of Bliss." *Time*, October 26, 1987, 118.

Scotto, Barbara. Review of *Leaving Home*. *Wilson Library Bulletin* 62.4(1987): 83–84.

Steinberg, Sybil. Review of *Leaving Home*. *Publishers Weekly*, August 28, 1987, 67.

We Are Still Married

Anderson, A. J. Review of *We Are Still Married*. *Library Journal*, April 1, 1989, 89–90.

Henderson, Bill. "Ordinary Folks, Repulsive and Otherwise." *The New York Times Book Review*, April 9, 1989, 13.

Korn, Eric. "Irritation Soars." *The Times Literary Supplement*, November 3–9, 1989, 1217.

Review of *We Are Still Married*. *The New Yorker*, December 18, 1989, 115.

Review of *We Are Still Married*. *Publishers Weekly*, February 24, 1989, 211.

Review of *We Are Still Married*. *Time*, May 15, 1989, 81.

WLT: A Radio Romance

Adler, Jerry. Review of *WLT: A Radio Romance*. *Newsweek*, November 18, 1991, 84.

Babcock, William A. "Garrison Keillor Writes about Radio's Dark Side." *Christian Science Monitor*, November 7, 1991, 13.

Bernays, Anne. "Radio Days." *The New York Times Book Review*, November 10, 1991, 24.

Beverly, Elizabeth. "Static on the Page." *Commonweal*, April 10, 1992, 26–27.

Dwyer, Victor. "Tuning in to America." *Maclean's*, November 25, 1991, 70.

Holston, Noel. "Keillor Says He's Freed His Characters." *Minneapolis Star Tribune*, November 17, 1991, F1+.

Kaveney, Roz. "Small-town Sentiments." *The Times Literary Supplement*, January 17, 1992, 24.

Naylor, Charles. "Of Mikes and Men." *The Nation*, December 23, 1991, 823–24.

Postlethwaite, Diane. "Is This Garrison?" *Minneapolis Star Tribune*, November 17, 1991, 12F.

Skow, John. "The Ghosts of Studio B." *Time*, November 25, 1991, 99–100.

Smiley, Jane. "Fiction in Review." *Yale Review* 81.1(1993): 148–62.

Spalding, Frances. Review of *WLT: A Radio Romance*. *Times Educational Supplement*, February 7, 1992, 29.

Review of *WLT: A Radio Romance*. *Publishers Weekly*, August 23, 1991, 47.

The Book of Guys

Adams, Robert M. "Boys Will Be Boys." *The New York Times Book Review*, January 13, 1994, 19.

Review of *The Book of Guys*. *Publishers Weekly*, September 20, 1993, 62.

Jeffreys, Susan. "Saddle Saws." *New Statesman and Society*, January 14, 1994, 40–41.

Shulman, Nicola. "The Strong Silent Type." *The Times Literary Supplement*, January 21, 1994, 19.

Skow, John. "Dionysus at 50 and More Woe." *Time*, November 22, 1993, 82.

Wright, A. J. Review of *The Book of Guys*. *Library Journal*, November 1, 1993, 151.

Zeidner, Lisa. "Why Is Marriage Like the Electoral College?" *The New York Times Book Review*, December 12, 1993, 13.

Wobegon Boy

Bartholomew, David. Review of *Wobegon Boy*. *Library Journal*, December 1997, 153.

Heard, Alex. Review of *Wobegon Boy*. *The New York Times Book Review*, October 26, 1997, 14–15.

Kontorovich, E. V. "Jefferson in Minnesota." *National Review*, December 8, 1997, 51–52.

Seaman, Donna. Review of *Wobegon Boy*. *Booklist*, October 1, 1997, 19.

Urquhart, James. "Trouble with Corn." *New Statesman*, May 22, 1998, 57.

Review of *Wobegon Boy*. *Publishers Weekly*, September 29, 1997, 66.

OTHER SECONDARY SOURCES

Aristotle. *On the Art of Fiction*. Translated by L. J. Potts. Cambridge: Cambridge University Press, 1959.

Atkins, Douglas G. *Reading Deconstruction: Deconstructive Reading*. Lexington: University Press of Kentucky, 1983.

Boyd, Frances, and David Quinn. *Stories from Lake Wobegon: Advanced Listening and Conversation Skills*. Preface by Garrison Keillor. New York: Longman, 1990.

Bressler, Charles E. *Literary Criticism: An Introduction to Theory and Practice*. 2d ed. Upper Saddle River: Prentice, 1999.

Chanady, Amaryll Beatrice. *Magical Realism and the Fantastic: Resolved Versus Unresolved Antimony*. New York: Garland, 1985.

Culler, Jonathan. *On Deconstruction: Theory and Criticism after Structuralism*. Ithaca: Cornell University Press, 1982.

de Beauvoir, Simone. *The Second Sex*. Translated by H. M. Parshley. 1952. Reprinted, New York: Vintage, 1974.

Faris, Wendy B. "Scheherazade's Children: Magical Realism and Postmodern Fiction." *Magical Realism: Theory, History, Community*. Edited by Lois Parkinson Zamora and Wendy B. Faris. Durham: Duke University Press, 1995, 163–90.

Flores, Angel. "Magical Realism in Spanish American Fiction." *Magical Realism: Theory, History, Community*. Edited by Lois Parkinson Zamora and Wendy B. Faris. Durham: Duke University Press, 1995, 109–17.

Franklin, Benjamin. "Remarks Concerning the Savages of North America." *The Norton Anthology of American Literature*. Shorter 4th ed. Edited by Nina Baym, et al. New York: Norton, 1995, 219–22.

Freud, Sigmund. *The Ego and the Id*. Translated by Joan Riviere. *The Major Works of Sigmund Freud*. Chicago: Encyclopaedia Britannica, 1952. Vol. 54 of *Great Books of the Western World*. Edited by Robert Maynard Hutchins. 54 vols.

Freud, Sigmund. *The Interpretation of Dreams*. Translated by A. A. Brill. *The Major Works of Sigmund Freud*. Chicago: Encyclopaedia Britannica, 1952. Vol. 54 of *Great Books of the Western World*. Edited by Robert Maynard Hutchins. 54 vols.

Galligan, Edward L. *The Comic Vision in Literature*. Athens: University of Georgia Press, 1984.

Gerber, John C. *Mark Twain*. Boston: Twayne, 1988.

Gilbert, Sandra M. "What Do Feminist Critics Want?" *The New Feminist Criticism: Essays on Women, Literature, and Theory*. Edited by Elaine Showalter. New York: Pantheon, 1985, 29–45.

Hall, Calvin S. *A Primer of Freudian Psychology*. New York: World Publication, 1954.

Harmon, William, and C. Hugh Holman. *A Handbook to Literature*. 7th ed. Upper Saddle River: Prentice, 1996.

Howells, William Dean. *My Mark Twain: Reminiscences and Criticisms*. New York: Harper, 1910.

"Humor." *Webster's Tenth New Collegiate Dictionary*. 1993 ed.

Koestler, Arthur. *The Act of Creation*. New York: Macmillan, 1964.

Leal, Luis. "Magical Realism in Spanish American Literature." Translated by Wendy B. Faris. *Magical Realism: Theory, History, Community*. Edited by Lois Parkinson Zamora and Wendy B. Faris. Durham: Duke University Press, 1995, 119–24.

Lynn, Steven. *Texts and Contexts: Writing About Literature with Critical Theory*. New York: HarperCollins, 1994.

MacHovec, Frank J. *Freud: His Contributions to Modern Thought*. Mount Vernon: Peter Pauper, 1973.

Nilsen, Don L. F. *Humor in American Literature: A Selected Annotated Bibliography*. New York: Garland, 1992.

Rogers, Will. *Letters of a Self-Made Diplomat to His President*. Edited by Joseph A. Stout, Jr. Stillwater: Oklahoma State University Press, 1977.

Roh, Franz. "Magical Realism: Post-Expressionism (1925)." Translated by Wendy B. Faris. *Magical Realism: Theory, History, Community*. Edited by Lois Parkinson Zamora and Wendy B. Faris. Durham: Duke University Press, 1995, 15–31.

Rosenblatt, Louise M. *Literature as Exploration*. New York: D. Appleton-Century, 1938.

Stevens, Bonnie Klomp, and Larry L. Stewart. *A Guide to Literary Criticism and Research*. 3d ed. Fort Worth: Harcourt, 1996.

Thurber, James. *Writings and Drawings*. Edited by Garrison Keillor. New York: Library of America, 1996.

Twain, Mark. *Mark Twain in Eruption*. Edited by Bernard DeVoto. 1922. Reprint, New York: Capricorn, 1968.

"Winfrey Frustrated with Springer." *Johnson City Press*, February 10, 1999, 9.

Yates, Norris W. *The American Humorist: Conscience of the Twentieth Century*. Ames: Iowa State University Press, 1964.

Index

About the Author

MARCIA SONGER is Assistant Professor of English at East Tennessee State University where she teaches European Literature, African Literature, and English as a Second Language. She has written numerous contributions to published works on Literature including chapters for *Great Women Mystery Writers: A Biocritical Dictionary* (Greenwood, 1994). She has also taught high school in the United States and in Saudi Arabia.

Critical Companions to Popular Contemporary Writers
Second Series

Rudolfo A. Anaya *by Margarite Fernandez Olmos*

Maya Angelou *by Mary Jane Lupton*

Louise Erdrich *by Lorena L. Stookey*

Ernest J. Gaines *by Karen Carmean*

John Irving *by Josie P. Campbell*

Jamaica Kincaid *by Lizabeth Paravisini-Gebert*

Barbara Kingsolver *by Mary Jean DeMarr*

Terry McMillan *by Paulette Richards*

Larry McMurtry *by John M. Reilly*

Toni Morrison *by Missy Dehn Kubitschek*

Amy Tan *by E. D. Huntley*

Anne Tyler *by Paul Bail*

Leon Uris *by Kathleen Shine Cain*

Critical Companions to Popular Contemporary Writers
First Series—*also available on CD-ROM*

V. C. Andrews
  by E. D. Huntley

Tom Clancy
  by Helen S. Garson

Mary Higgins Clark
  by Linda C. Pelzer

Arthur C. Clarke
  by Robin Anne Reid

James Clavell
  by Gina Macdonald

Pat Conroy
  by Landon C. Burns

Robin Cook
  by Lorena Laura Stookey

Michael Crichton
  by Elizabeth A. Trembley

Howard Fast
  by Andrew Macdonald

Ken Follett
  by Richard C. Turner

John Grisham
  by Mary Beth Pringle

James Herriot
  by Michael J. Rossi

Tony Hillerman
  by John M. Reilly

John Jakes
  by Mary Ellen Jones

Stephen King
  by Sharon A. Russell

Dean Koontz
  by Joan G. Kotker

Robert Ludlum
  by Gina Macdonald

Anne McCaffrey
  by Robin Roberts

Colleen McCullough
  by Mary Jean DeMarr

James A. Michener
  by Marilyn S. Severson

Anne Rice
  by Jennifer Smith

Tom Robbins
  *by Catherine E. Hoyser and
  Lorena Laura Stookey*

John Saul
  by Paul Bail

Erich Segal
  by Linda C. Pelzer

Gore Vidal
  *by Susan Baker and
  Curtis S. Gibson*